Also from (

Making the Choice
When Typical School Doesn't Fit Your Atypical Child

Forging Paths
Beyond Traditional Schooling

If This is a Gift, Can I Send it Back?
Surviving in the Land of the Gifted and Twice Exceptional

Learning in the 21st Century
How to Connect, Collaborate, and Create

How to Work and Homeschool
Practical Tips, Advice, and Strategies from Parents

Educating Your Gifted Child
How One Public School Teacher Embraced Homeschooling

Self-Directed Learning
Documentation and Life Stories

Gifted, Bullied, Resilient
A Brief Guide for Smart Families

Writing Your Own Script
A Parent's Role in the Gifted Child's Social Development

Micro-Schools
Creating Personalized Learning on a Budget

Your Rainforest Mind
A Guide to the Well-Being of Gifted Adults and Youth

Coming Soon from GHF Press

Kathleen Humble
Gifted Myths

Kelly Hirt
Twelve Ways to Lift Up Our Twice-Exceptional Children

Joy Navan
Gifted Elders

From Home Education to Higher Education

A Guide for Recruiting, Assessing, and Supporting Homeschooled Applicants

By Lori Dunlap

Published by GHF Press

A Division of Gifted Homeschoolers Forum

3701 Pacific Ave. SE - PMB #609

Olympia, WA 98501

ISBN-13: 978-0692902592 (GHF Press)

ISBN-10: 0692902597

Cover design by Shawn Keehne

www.shawnkeehne.com • skeehne@mac.com

Dedication

I am so grateful to my family for all their patience and support during the research and writing of this book. I am particularly grateful to my husband, Dave, and our two boys, Sam and Ben, for their regular words of encouragement, hugs, and willingness to take over even more of the daily chores so I could have time to write. I know there were times when they thought this writing project might never be done, and that my exclamations of "I have to go write!" would never end, but they remained completely supportive throughout, and I cannot thank them enough.

Table of Contents

Introduction

The audacity of some people is unbelievable. As I sat flipping through the file one more time, still in disbelief that someone could be so bold, could so flagrantly flaunt the admissions process like this, I decided we needed to do something about it. I was accustomed to seeing applications that I suspected of being "padded," of stretching the truth, but this application had reached a new level. I needed to talk to the admissions director—she was also reading the file—and together we would figure out how to respond. We just could not let this applicant get away with including false information on a graduate school application. This was entirely unacceptable.

My feelings approached the level of righteous indignation as I walked over to the admissions office and reflected on the details of the file, particularly the applicant's resume. Did this student think we would believe that, by the age of eighteen, before she even entered college, she had published two books and started not only a newspaper business, but a nonprofit organization as well? There was no way we would admit someone so deceptive. As the director of the Office of Career Development, how could I possibly help find a job for someone with such low morals?

Maria, the director of admissions, shook her head vigorously as we talked, agreeing that there was no way we could just let this go. We decided that a phone call with the applicant was in order, and that Maria should be the one to confront her. She said she would follow up with me after the call and let me know how it had gone. I could hardly wait to hear. However, when Maria walked into my office a couple of days later, the look on her face was entirely different—gone were the furrowed brow and set jaw. She was still shaking her head, but much more slowly now. Mostly, she just looked kind of confused. "I talked to that applicant," she said. "Everything on her resume is true. She was homeschooled." What? Homeschooled?

Until that moment, I'm not even sure I had ever heard the term "homeschooled." I had certainly never met anyone who had been educated this way, at least not that I knew of. Everyone I had ever known had gone to a public or private school, graduated, and then gone on to college or a job. No exceptions. In retrospect, given that this was in 2007 and I was the mother of two young boys (one already in school), it is hard to imagine how I was so unaware of an education movement that already had at least 1.5 million members, and about which so much research had already been conducted. Even harder to imagine is how I might have responded if someone had told me that in just a few short years, I would be homeschooling both of my boys.

A Closer Look

Homeschooling is an even more common educational path these days than it was during my first exposure to the idea just ten years ago. Per the 2012 National Home Education Survey conducted by the

National Center for Education Statistics (NCES),[1] in 2012 approximately 1.8 million children in the United States were being educated at home, representing about 3.5 percent of all students between the ages of five and seventeen. As of 2016 and the writing of this book, many estimates put the current number closer to 2.5 million. Homeschoolers are notoriously difficult to count, though, because they are not all in one place or easily identified, so estimates vary widely. Regardless of the actual total, everyone agrees that this number has been growing at an accelerated rate over the past decade, increasing by seven to ten percent per year, which makes homeschooling the fastest growing form of education in the country. This means that since 1999, when the federal government first started collecting information about homeschooling, the number of homeschoolers in the United States has doubled. And for several individual states, the change has been even more dramatic. In North Carolina, for example, as the new national curriculum has been introduced along with an increased emphasis on testing, so many families have pulled their children out of school that in 2014 the number of homeschooled students surpassed the number of students enrolled in private schools—a twenty-seven percent increase in just two years.

What is driving so many families to a route so different from how their parents and grandparents were educated? According to the same NCES research, twenty-five percent of homeschooled students have parents who say that their concerns about the school environment was their primary motivation for homeschooling their child, and ninety-one percent say that school environment was at least one of the reasons they chose to homeschool. The second- and third-most cited reasons are "other reasons," which include family travel or living a long distance from the closest schools, and "dissatisfaction with academic instruction." The desire to provide religious instruction is the primary reason for homeschooling for only sixteen percent of the respondents. If this latter piece of information comes as a surprise to you, you are not alone.

In the 1980s and 1990s, as the homeschooling movement began to gain momentum initiated by the early advocates of homeschooling from the 1960s and 1970s, many of the "early adopters" of homeschooling made the choice because they wanted to provide religious instruction as part of their children's education. Thus, many observers outside of the homeschooling community continue to believe that homeschoolers are primarily religious. In actuality, statistics show that for the past couple of decades, as the educational system in the United States has struggled, and as technology has facilitated the access to more alternative educational options, an increasing number of families are opting out of the traditional educational system for primarily non-religious reasons.

Another misconception of the homeschooling community centers around the education levels of the parents, who are often assumed to be primarily wealthy and highly educated. In fact, the demographic data of homeschooling parents as collected and reported by NCES shows that these parents are remarkably average—they have essentially the same level of education and income as all other parents of school-aged children, with just more than half having some college education or a bachelor's degree. [2]

Given the size and momentum of the movement, along with the continuing controversy about the failings of our current public education system, it seems reasonable to predict that the homeschooling community is likely to continue its impressive growth rate. Further fueling this expansion is the increasing number of reports on how well homeschoolers are performing on standardized academic tests. According to the National Home Education Research Institute (NHERI) and other homeschool research and advocacy organizations, homeschoolers tend to score well above the national average on standardized achievement tests, including the SAT and ACT.[3] While there is some controversy about exactly how much better homeschoolers perform (many of the studies do not include a random sampling of homeschoolers, but rather a self-selected group of respondents), most show that homeschooled students typically score in the sixtieth to eightieth percentiles. Multiple factors likely contribute to this outcome, including high levels of parental involvement and one-on-one interactions with outside instructors and tutors.

Implications for Higher Education

The implications of this trend are undeniably significant for both public and private K-12 schools and policy makers, but they are also significant for higher education institutions, most of which can expect to see an increase in the number of applicants from this non-traditional background in the near future (if they have not already). According to Dr. Brian Ray, a home education researcher at the National Home Education Research Institute (NHERI), we can:

> [E]xpect to observe a notable surge in the number of children being homeschooled in the next five to ten years. The rise would be in terms of both absolute numbers and percentage of the K to 12

student population. This increase would be in part because of the reasonable possibility that a large number of those individuals who were being home educated in the 1990s may begin to homeschool their own school-age children and the continued successes of home-educated students.[4]

In other words, home-educated students who are applying to college now are just the first wave of homeschooled applicants who will be pursuing higher education in the coming years.

What's more, a higher-than-average percentage of homeschoolers choose to pursue higher education, with some estimates showing that at least fifty percent of homeschooled students attend college (others indicate that more than seventy percent of homeschoolers pursue some form of higher education), compared to forty-six percent of the general US population. So, as the total number of homeschoolers continues to increase, the percentage of applications from homeschoolers as a portion of total applications is also likely to increase. Given the variety of reasons that families choose to homeschool, multiplied by the wide range of approaches to homeschooling and the infinite number of unique educational opportunities and accomplishments of these students, those working in higher education admissions may begin to feel overwhelmed by the number and complexity of these applications, wondering how best to assess an increasing number of applications from students who do not have traditional transcripts, course descriptions, or GPAs.

Likewise, as more homeschooled students appear on campus and in college classrooms, staff and faculty may begin to notice different levels of engagement and diverse requests and expectations from these non-traditional students. Homeschooled students are generally accustomed to actively directing their education, which means that they tend to ask more questions and are more comfortable challenging assumptions. This will likely be a mixed blessing for many in higher education as they adapt to these new dynamics and demands.

Developing a plan to recruit, assess, and assimilate this population is a worthwhile investment of time. Staff and faculty at colleges and universities who have already worked with homeschooled students have noticed that these are particularly motivated, thoughtful, and creative students. They have had time to pursue their unique interests, dive deeply into their passions, learn how to navigate ambiguity, and develop personal attributes like grit and resilience. They attend college because higher

> *Of course, there comes a point when even the most self-directed learner can use guidance from scholarly instructors. When high-achieving homeschoolers reach that threshold, many look to top-tier colleges and universities. In competing for admission, they want the same sort of academic recognition enjoyed by their more conventionally educated peers, even though they're short on formal credentials.*
>
> ~Christine Foster,
> "In a Class by Themselves,"
> Stanford Alumni Newsletter. Nov/Dec 2000

education aligns with their long-term vision for their life, not because they do not know what else to do after high school. And research shows that they are at least as likely, if not more likely, to graduate from college as traditional students, and continue to succeed even after graduation, many continuing on to start their own businesses or to excel in many other fields.[5] So, as the total number of high school graduates is set to plateau over the next decade and as average yield rates at four-year colleges continue to decline, many higher education institutions are recognizing that homeschooled students represent an ideal target audience for recruitment.

Implications for Homeschooling Families

As the number of homeschoolers continues to increase, and as more of these students begin applying to colleges and universities, homeschooling families need to be aware of the implications. Though this lifestyle is rapidly becoming more recognized and accepted, in terms of standing out in your admissions application, as one college admissions officer said, "Being homeschooled doesn't make you interesting anymore." So, as part of your college planning you need to invest additional time in highlighting what makes you interesting and distinctive beyond just having been homeschooled. You need to communicate what you have done to fully maximize the freedom and flexibility that comes with homeschooling, and show how you have used this opportunity to pursue your unique interests.

Now, more than ever, admissions officers face exceptional challenges when reviewing non-traditional applications like yours. In speaking with dozens of professionals involved in college admissions, most clearly want to understand homeschoolers' particular experiences and qualifications, but find it very difficult to do when they have stacks of admissions files to review every year. We can help them help our students by developing very clear descriptions of our homeschooling philosophy and approach, asking clear and concise questions, providing thorough transcripts and course descriptions, and addressing the key concerns about homeschoolers that persist outside of the homeschooling community. We will explore ideas for how to approach each of these in the coming chapters.

A Quick Preview

While I hope that anyone who is interested in helping homeschooled students pursue their goals in higher education will find the ideas and information in this book valuable, I have written it especially for the two groups who have a clear and vested interest in increasing college access and admissions for homeschooled students:

1. Professionals who counsel, recruit, assess, and teach homeschooled students at the college level, including independent college advisors, admissions readers and interviewers, admissions officers, and higher education staff and faculty
2. Homeschooling families

In short, if your professional role includes working with homeschoolers seeking higher education, this book will update you on current trends, clarify different educational choices and approaches, and support you by sharing common and best practices among the admissions community. Whether you directly advise and counsel these students through the college selection and application process, work within a college or university considering homeschoolers' applications for admission, or are a faculty member who teaches homeschoolers or occasionally supports the admissions process, you will find the information you need in the following chapters to more fully understand this population, along with some suggested strategies and approaches for easily and effectively connecting with, engaging, and assessing these non-traditional students.

If you are a homeschooling parent or student, this book holds much for you as well. As you help your child develop the knowledge and skills necessary for a successful life, and as you begin to plan for college as part of this path, you need to understand the perspectives and challenges of those who will be reviewing your child's application and, ultimately, teaching her or him. In addition, if you decide to work with an independent college advisor at the beginning of the application process, be prepared to assist him or her in understanding your homeschooling experience, as even highly experienced advisors may not have worked with many homeschoolers. This book will provide you with some ideas and recommendations for succinctly describing your educational approach, effectively demonstrating your child's educational accomplishments and qualifications, and strategically positioning your child for acceptance to the colleges of her or his choice.

To ensure that all readers have a thorough and updated perspective of the homeschooling movement, I have dedicated the first three chapters to providing an overview of homeschooling, including the personal stories of several homeschooling families. Chapter One provides a detailed discussion of the factors that drive so many families to choose homeschooling these days, along with descriptions of typical and special homeschooling populations. Chapter Two proposes a model that visually represents the different approaches to homeschooling, including profiles of representative students and families, while Chapter Three offers a closer examination of common homeschooling myths and stereotypes. You may wonder if this level of explanation is necessary. I believe it is. Given the diversity of homeschoolers, multiplied by a large (and growing) number of non-traditional educational tools and opportunities they have selected, cultivating a current and accurate perspective of these students' experiences and world views is essential if you hope to effectively engage with them. If you are a homeschooling parent, these chapters will provide you with ideas of how to describe your educational choices to college admissions officers, and even to others you encounter who are interested.

As outdated stereotypes of homeschoolers persist in our country, many parents and students have consistently felt misunderstood and frustrated. As one parent recently shared with me, "Instead of viewing homeschoolers as sheltered, insular, and lacking socialization, people should consider the possibility that they are actual better socialized and more mature than others in their age group." To that end, in Chapter Four I share and discuss specific questions and concerns homeschooling parents across the country submitted in a 2015-2016 survey about the transition to higher education, including a variety of messages they asked me to pass along to those in higher education. Additionally, we take a "peek behind the curtain" of college admissions with a close look at the perspectives and insights of almost sixty admissions officers derived from a separate national survey of admission professionals conducted in 2015. This chapter is guaranteed to offer helpful and actionable insights for everyone.

In Chapters Five and Six, I provide several ideas of what you can expect from homeschooled students in the classroom (and what they are expecting from you), how they typically adjust to college life, and numerous suggestions on how best to engage and motivate them. This information is pulled from published research, as well as recent interviews I conducted with admissions officers. I also describe some best practices research for attracting and assessing homeschoolers conducted among a select group of admissions officers, and provide a series of recommendations and conclusions in the final chapter.

My hope is that the information and ideas offered in this book will broaden and strengthen the bridge that already exists between the homeschooling community and the higher education community. While this connection is sometimes difficult to navigate for both sides, with the right information and the right connection points, the process can be facilitated for both. The intended result is that many more colleges and universities will successfully recruit more of these highly engaged and motivated students, and that many more homeschoolers will be accepted to their top-choice schools.

Chapter One

Who Homeschools and Why

The moment I spotted him struggling to squeeze through the double glass doors, I could tell it had been another difficult day. His unzipped backpack, gaping open and hanging by the strap from one arm, with his loose papers and lunch box precariously clutched under the other, gave the appearance that he was literally coming undone. As he stumbled out from behind a cluster of charging, chattering six-year-olds who were racing onto the front lawn "pick up" area, my suspicions were further confirmed when I spotted the moist, wrinkled neckline of his T-shirt—a clear indication that his recently-developed nervous chewing habit was in full effect. When he drew closer, I smiled as brightly as I could and optimistically asked, "How was your day, buddy?" "Not good, Mama," came the weary reply. "Can we just go home?" The pleading look in his huge, chocolate-brown eyes clearly signaled that he was trying to hold himself together. I knew better than to push or to ask anything more—we'd been here before.

Once we arrived home and settled at the table with a snack, I asked what had happened. Eyes brimming with tears, chin quivering defiantly, he told me about a math lesson the teacher had presented to the class that day. "I could hear the words coming out of her mouth, but I couldn't understand what she was saying," he explained as the tears finally spilled over, slipping down his round, peach-fuzz cheeks. In short, he had not understood the lesson or what he was supposed to do. His eager-to-please disposition caused him to become very anxious and, when the other kids at the table started to notice, he felt embarrassed and even more upset. When he headed to the reading corner to calm down, his teacher decided he was disrupting the class (as she informed me the next day in the meeting I requested), so she pulled him out of the classroom and into the hallway. What she clearly had not understood was that my son would have calmed himself down if he had been left alone for a little while, and by drawing more attention to him, she had made the situation much more distressing than my six-year-old was able to cope with on his own.

This was not the first time my son had come home upset and confused from first grade. He had such wonderful preschool and kindergarten experiences, that we were all scrambling to figure out what was happening, why things were so different this year. He was academically capable when I helped him with homework in the evenings, but the increased pressure to perform in the classroom was making him anxious and emotional. As I discussed the situation on the phone with my mom, an elementary school teacher in another state, she said something that would fundamentally change our lives for at least the next twelve years: "Do we have to have the homeschooling discussion again?"

I had forgotten until that moment that we had considered the idea of homeschooling a few years earlier, when my older son was in first grade and also struggling. Now that he was in fourth grade, my husband

and I were both noticing that the spark he had had before starting school was completely gone. His ravenous desire to learn the names of all the dinosaurs, to construct detailed clay models, to create intricate and imaginative stories starring his stuffed animals, had long since disappeared. Now, our ten-year-old was the quiet "please don't notice me" kind of kid at school during the day, who frequently cried in frustration about the overwhelming amount of homework he needed to do at night. It was clear that neither of my boys was thriving in school and, in fact, both were losing their curiosity about the world, their love of learning new things, their smiles. For years we had worked closely with the teachers and schools, trying everything we could think of to make things work and hoping that things would get better. But now we decided it was time to do something radically different: pull them out of school.

Why Homeschooling?

Our homeschooling story is not unusual. As the NCES research cited earlier shows, a majority of families who make the decision to educate their children at home do so because the traditional school structure and environment clearly does not serve their children. And if we look deeper into these numbers, by talking to parents directly and reading additional research, we find more explicit information about the primary reasons parents are leaving the school system. For example, many parents say that they are increasingly concerned about growing classroom sizes, developmentally inappropriate instructional methods, and increased emphasis on high-stakes testing and the corresponding increase in time spent on test preparation in the classroom. With respect to the social environment, parents cite peer pressure, drugs, and incidents of bullying as the catalysts for making the change.

Looking more closely at some special populations within the homeschooling community highlights other motivating factors even more clearly. For example, a growing number of families of color are choosing to homeschool, mentioning the disparities and inequalities their children have experienced in the classroom, both subtle and overt, as the primary reason. In fact, African American families are one of the fastest-growing segments within the homeschooling community. According to research conducted by Ama Mazama, a professor at Temple University, approximately 220,000 African American families currently educate their children at home,[1] representing about ten percent of the total homeschooling population. In an interview with *The Atlantic*, Professor Mazama explained, "Whenever there are mentions of African American homeschoolers, it's assumed that we homeschool for the same reasons as European American homeschoolers, but this isn't really the case."[2] As part of a 2012 survey of African American homeschooling families, she found that "racial protectionism"—protecting their children from racism at school—was a significant factor for many parents, as were "Euro-centric" history classes and a culture of low expectations for African American students.

Other research efforts also support the assertion that differences exist in the educational experiences and opportunities for children of color. Recent national research concludes that African American and Hispanic students have less access to high level math and science classes, are more likely to have less experienced teachers in their schools, and are more likely to be harshly disciplined or suspended from school. Per one federal report, "Black children accounted for nineteen percent of all preschool students in 2013-2014, but they made up forty-seven percent of those who received suspensions."[3] What's more, reports indicate that in more than one third of bullying cases, race was an issue.

Other special populations within the homeschooling community cite learning or emotional needs not accommodated effectively in the classroom as their primary reason for homeschooling. This includes gifted

> *Depicting all homeschoolers as anti-school would be an unfortunate mischaracterization. Some homeschooling families do make ideological choices about how to educate their children, but far more leave their neighborhood public schools, originally chosen by default, because the public school system does not or cannot meet the needs of their children.*
>
> ~"US Public Education Policy: Missing Voices"[4]

students, many of whom leave traditional schools because they are not sufficiently challenged at school, and frequently because of social difficulties they face, like feelings of not fitting in with their peers, or feelings of loneliness and isolation. For gifted kids who commonly exhibit emotional and intellectual intensity, or "overexcitabilities," relating to teachers and friends who do not understand them leads to even deeper feelings of disconnect in the school environment, often resulting in declining academic performance, and a need for their parents to intervene while confronting their own views about education. As one mother of two highly gifted children explains, "I have learned how to shift my views from a traditional mindset into a progressive freethinker, which is exactly what my intense children demanded of me."

Parents of students with learning disabilities, and parents of students who are both gifted *and* diagnosed with a learning disability (often referred to as "twice exceptional" or "2e") also report frustration about insufficient academic support as well as significant social problems as the leading factors in their decision to homeschool. Many parents of students with learning disabilities actually say that "too much focus" on their child's disabilities was a problem for them, highlighting what their child could *not* do rather than what they could, and reinforcing the idea that they were not smart or capable. For twice-exceptional kids, their asynchronous development compounds the issues—they excel in some areas, but are behind their peers in others.

This was the case for Korie, who made the decision to homeschool her son, Max, just a few weeks into third grade. While Max was clearly gifted, having taught himself to read in kindergarten, school had nonetheless always been a struggle for him. He did not struggle with learning or intellectual issues, but with social ones. Max just could not seem to connect with other kids and often experienced teasing, occasionally even bullying. In first grade he was diagnosed with clinical depression, and also with Attention Deficit and Hyperactivity Disorder (ADHD), qualifying him as "twice-exceptional."

Medication and a supportive teacher helped Max through second grade, but things were still difficult. As Korie explains, "His teacher and the school principal tried, but they just did not seem to get him." Also, the school had very few resources for working with a boy like Max, and the school psychologist who was brought in to help "was just horrible, and so out of touch," says Korie. "He was only focused on how to get Max to behave. It was not about what was best for my son."

Around this time Korie began thinking about the possibility of homeschooling. She started reading lots of books and attended an information session provided by a state-wide homeschool organization, but decided to keep Max in school for third grade, again hoping for the best. Just several weeks after the first day of school, however, social issues once again became a problem. Max had become the target for kids who regularly accused him of misbehaviors that Max claimed he had not done. "It seemed to have become a pattern," says Korie.

One day, I was sitting in front of his teacher feeling so tired, I hadn't even taken a shower, and as I looked at this young woman, I just knew it wasn't going to work. I told her right then that I was going to homeschool Max, and just left.

Max has now been homeschooled for several years, and Korie says she will never send him back to a public school. He is happy and has a lot of freedom to pursue his interests, which include just about anything involving science. Max spends a lot of time taking science classes with a variety of organizations in their area, in addition to attending regular weekly meetings with a homeschool co-op, which is where he met his current best friend. As Korie explains, "Homeschool kids feel a level of freedom that other kids don't even know is available. And they're allowed to be comfortable with who they are."

The challenges of traditional school are not limited to ethnic minorities or students with learning difference. Many students of all types and backgrounds struggle in school, and some suffer very real consequences as a result. Kirsten Olson, educational researcher and president of the board of directors of the Institute for Democratic Education in America (IDEA), even goes so far as to call these negative effective of traditional schooling "wounds." Her book, *Wounded by School: Recapturing the Joy of Learning and Standing up to Old School Culture*, is the result of research that she undertook to learn about the *positive* effects of school had had on people's lives. Instead, she found that rather than recalling their school experiences fondly, the people she interviewed actually had memories of pain, disappointment, and frustration. After interviewing people of all different ages, from school kids to grandparents, and from a wide variety of backgrounds, Dr. Olson categorized the wounds people experienced into seven different groups, and described the resulting consequences, including a diminished capacity for imagination and creativity, lack of comfort with risk-taking, loss of intellectual enthusiasm, and the choosing of narrower life paths.

Many parents who decide to homeschool their own children do so because they want to protect their children from suffering the same wounds and resulting effects that they suffered during their educational experiences. Speaking with groups of homeschooling parents, it is not unusual to hear things like, "In retrospect, I don't know how I made it through that time," or, "I would never want to go back and go through that again." Most of these parents finished school before the current emphasis on standardized testing had taken hold, and yet their memories still evoke strong emotions, and sometimes wry laughter, as they recall acting against the rules and rebelling against the constraints and requirements imposed on them. As one dad relates:

> *I barely graduated from high school. I think some of my teachers*
> *gave me a "D" just to get me out of there. It took me a long time*

28

after finishing school to realize I wasn't a stupid person—I'm intelligent in different ways than they wanted me to be in school.

The Benefits of Homeschooling

As the homeschooling movement grows, success stories and research results are more widely and frequently shared. Consequently, many families are deciding to educate their children at home for one reason that the statistics do not capture—the *benefits* of homeschooling. These parents, some of whom opted not to enroll their children in school in the first place, believe their children will develop into happier, more well-rounded adults if they are actively involved in making the types of choices about their education and growth that they could not make if they were in school. Parents are weighing their children's social and emotional development equally with their intellectual advancement.

> **Commonly Reported Benefits of Homeschooling:**
>
> Closer family connections
> Freedom to pursue interests
> Love of learning/deeper learning
> Time for community involvement
> More connection with the real world
> Interactions with people of all ages

These social and emotional benefits of homeschooling were the focus of several of the early homeschooling advocates and thought leaders of the 1960s and 1970s, most notably, John Holt. As an educator and author of several prominent books including *How Children Learn*, *Learning All the Time,* and *Teach Your Own: The John Holt Book of Homeschooling* (co-authored with Pat Farenga), Holt was one of the earliest and most ardent proponents of homeschooling, and remains one of the most influential to this day, despite his death decades ago. Although he valued and discussed learning and intellectual development, his major emphasis was the fundamental importance of the social environment in providing children with the "freedom, choice, and self-direction" they need before meaningful learning can happen. He encouraged parents to homeschool their children right from the beginning, to avoid enrolling in school entirely, and, in *Teach Your Own*, he answers the question, "Why do people take or keep their children out of school?":

> *Mostly for three reasons: they think that raising their children is their business, not the government's; they enjoy being with their children and watching and helping them learn, and don't want to give that up to others; they want to keep them from being hurt, mentally, physically, and spiritually.*

Although the counter-culture feel of the 1960s is clearly reflected in his response, these reasons continue to resonate today, with many homeschooling parents enthusiastically describing the benefits of this lifestyle, including enjoying being with their children and growing much closer as a family (if their children were previously in traditional school). Even parents who are homeschooling teenagers report close relationships with their children, challenging the assumption that the teenage angst and rebellion we often assume are a natural and required part of growing up actually may not be. As one parent explained:

> *With no pressure to conform or fit in, a major issue for many of my friends' kids who go to public school, there is also no need for*

rebellion. And as my kids have gotten older, our relationships have become closer and homeschooling has become even easier.

Many parents also cite "protecting their child's natural love of learning" as one of their primary motives for homeschooling. We all know that when we learn something because we choose to, are interested, or have a need to learn it, the new knowledge and skills stay with us indefinitely. Research has shown again and again that learners who are intrinsically motivated learn faster, are more persistent in working

> *Education is out of sync with what we know about how people learn. Sending my kids to school would disrupt their education.*
>
> ~Jen, homeschooling mother of two

through problems, enjoy the learning process more, and retain the information longer. This holds true for children as well as adults. As Matthew Lieberman, a professor and researcher at UCLA, reports, "For more than 75 years, studies have consistently found that only a small fraction of what is learned in the classroom is retained even a year after learning."[5] Why? Because the work done in the classroom that has little or no relevance to students' interests or daily lives. This is where homeschooling stands apart—regardless of the particular philosophy or method of homeschooling a family chooses, almost every homeschooler has a higher level of freedom to direct their education than if they had stayed in traditional school, and this freedom usually leads to intellectual vitality and a life-long love of learning.

But how do the students feel about being homeschooled? Are these just ideas that sound great, but do not actually work in practice? We hear regularly from parents and homeschooling experts about the reasons and benefits, but rarely from the students themselves. Do they think homeschooling was a good option for them, or do they feel like they have been disadvantaged or missed out on something? Sue Patterson, a well-known homeschooling mother, coach, and author, decided to investigate. For her most recent book, *Homeschooled Teens*, she surveyed seventy-five teens and young adults about their homeschooling experiences and perceptions, and found that the overwhelming majority of comments were positive and fell into six main categories:

1. They have a happier approach to learning.
2. They have been exposed to real world opportunities.
3. They have the freedom to make choices.
4. They have been able to avoid unnecessary stress.
5. Their socialization opportunities are better.
6. They have better influences.

As Mike, a sixteen-year-old participant in the *Homeschooled Teens* survey, reported:

I think one of the many advantages is learning how to choose what's best for [you]. Some people I know who have a more heavily structured education don't seem to have much passion for one subject over another. I also think that having more time to reflect and think about everything gives me a deeper connection. I feel like all of my current relationships with my family and friends are healthier than those of other teens.

Another young survey participant, Katie, age twenty-four, focused on the learning benefits of her experience:

I found that I still have a love of learning that many people I have met who went to a public school don't have. I never learned to hate learning and, being homeschooled, I have the tools at my disposal to learn anyhow and anywhere instead of just in a classroom with a teacher.

The word "engagement" is a word more frequently used by educational researchers than it is by parents or homeschoolers, but many of the benefits of homeschooling essentially boil down to this concept. Pursuing interests, diving deeply into passions, and developing an enthusiasm for learning are the core elements of engagement, a characteristic that seems to describe most homeschoolers. We will explore the concept of engagement more thoroughly in a later chapter, but briefly, many students who attend regular schools are not engaged, as Gallup found out in their 2014 Gallup Student Poll.[6] In short, they report that forty-seven percent of students in the United States are either "not engaged" or "actively disengaged" in school. On a five-point scale, eleventh and twelfth grade students average a 3.72 on the engagement scale, down from an average of 4.37 in fifth grade. While this type of research has not specifically been conducted with homeschoolers, based on an abundance of anecdotal evidence, it seems highly likely that engagement scores would be significantly higher for those educated at home who have the opportunity and freedom to "do what I do best every day."

Conclusion

So, closer family ties, a love of learning, and the freedom to pursue knowledge and skills that are interesting and relevant are some of the most frequently-cited advantages of homeschooling among homeschoolers, regardless of their age or their initial reasons for choosing this lifestyle. This does not mean that all families share similar philosophies or choose similar educational methods. In fact, with the considerable numbers of reasons and goals for homeschooling, the advancement of technology, a rapidly expanding supply of resources, and the growing momentum of the movement over the past two decades, options and opportunities abound, and every homeschooling experience looks different. While this offers a wonderful situation for families, it presents a problem for college admissions counselors and higher education staff and faculty who are trying to determine whether a homeschooled applicant can be successful at their school, or who need to compare the experiences and capabilities of several homeschooled students. So, let us get a clearer picture by taking a look at some different approaches to and specific examples of homeschooling.

Chapter Two

What Homeschooling Really Is, and Isn't

In order to begin to make sense of a homeschooler's non-traditional experiences and accomplishments, we must have a basic understanding of the range of homeschooling approaches. Because homeschoolers are typically counted and discussed as one group, many assume that families essentially do the same thing every day—some version of "school at home." Those unfamiliar with home education may have a vision of a mother and her children sitting at the kitchen table, textbooks open, worksheets and pencils at hand. In fact, for most families this image could not be further from the truth. The one and only thing we can accurately say that all homeschoolers have in common is that their children do not attend a public or private school full-time. This means that some students who are counted as homeschoolers do attend a traditional public or private school part-time, while others follow a standard curriculum with a full-time schedule at home, and yet others do nothing resembling school at all. If we could peek through the windows of ten, or even a hundred, homeschoolers at exactly the same time on a typical day, each family would be doing something completely different (and many of them would not even be home).

Adding to this complexity is the fact that most homeschoolers change what they do over time. What they are doing this year is not what they did last year, and it may change again next month. Many parents who are new to homeschooling opt for the "school at home" approach in the beginning because it fits with their idea of what education is. Over time, however, as they learn more from other experienced homeschoolers, and as they begin to notice how much their children learn on their own, they tend to relax and move away from their initial highly structured approach toward a more supervisory role. Conversely, other families feel comfortable jumping directly into "unschooling" (a term created by John Holt), which imposes very little structure and does not use any fixed curriculum, allowing children a significant amount of freedom to direct their own learning and activities.

Examples of Homeschooling Approaches and Philosophies:

Charlotte Mason
Classical
Eclectic
Montessori
Thomas Jefferson
Traditional ("school at home")
Unit Studies
Unschooling
Waldorf

So, with such a wide variety of options and approaches to educating children at home, how can someone fully understand and assess the knowledge, skills, and personal attributes of a given homeschooled student? First, I recommend thinking about homeschooling as a continuum, ranging from highly structured to completely unstructured. School-at-home is on the more-structured end, unschooling on the less-structured, with the middle incorporating a mix of some structure and some self-directed pursuits, or an eclectic approach.

Homeschooling Continuum

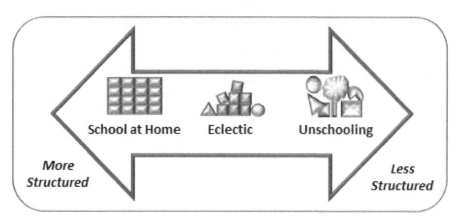

Each of these three primary categories contains considerable variation. Furthermore, homeschoolers across the spectrum incorporate well-known educational approaches like Waldorf, Montessori, or Charlotte Mason, but they often borrow selectively and add their own twist. Consequently, while a model of homeschooling can help provide some clarity, it can never really be more than a template—too many possible variations exist. Still, the model provides a foundation, a general framework, from which to ask questions. So, let us delve a little more into each general approach and meet a few representative families.

Highly Structured: "School at Home"

This approach most resembles school and is the easiest for people outside of the homeschooling community to understand. Families who adopt this philosophy of homeschooling often enroll in online charter or online private schools, frequently referred to as "virtual schools," or purchase a packaged curriculum that incorporates all lessons for all traditional school subjects, usually including the books, workbooks, science and art kits, and other materials. Some parents may choose to piece together their own curriculum, pulling different subjects from different sources depending on what they feel is the best fit for their child. The teacher may be a certified teacher employed by the virtual school, or the parent or a tutor may fill that role, but what they all have in common is the routine use of a standard curriculum for traditional subjects.

Virtual schools have quickly become a favorite choice of many homeschoolers. During the 2010-2011 school year, an estimated 250,000 K-12 students were enrolled full-time in online schools. Public charter schools, like those established by K12, Inc. and Connections Academy, are supported by tax dollars (levels of public funding vary by state)—making them essentially free to many students—providing textbooks, art supplies, and science equipment at no charge for the school year. Private online schools, like Oak Meadow and Laurel Springs, are comparable to standard private schools in that they charge tuition, but usually at a much lower rate than traditional private schools. Both charter and private virtual schools offer a variety of class options, particularly at the high school level, including AP and honors courses, and support students through online lectures and teacher contact by email or phone. Many of these schools even offer social opportunities through online clubs and local events for students who live in the same area.

In addition to full-time enrollment, virtual public and private schools generally offer part-time enrollment options. Full-time students receive a standard transcript upon graduation (very similar to a regular high school transcript), and part-time students generally receive grades and written teacher reviews at the end of each course. Regardless of whether a student attends full-time or part-time, however, the benefits of "attending" online schools are significant—the curriculum ensures that homeschooled students "keep up" with their in-school peers, and parents can be in the role of facilitator or advisor without taking on planning or teaching responsibilities. Also, for students who are college-bound, parents do not need to worry about grading, creating transcripts, or tracking their child's progress toward state graduation requirements.

On the other hand, some families do see a downside to virtual schools. Numerous parents observed that their children need to spend a lot of time sitting at the computer as they watch lectures, participate in virtual discussions, conduct research, and complete assignments. Other commonly-report concerns include the time it takes for even the most responsive teachers to reply to an email or voicemail question, assignments not easily tailored to students' interests or needs, and virtual schools' tendency to follow standard school schedules, limiting flexibility. One of the biggest issues, though, relates specifically to the public charter schools: they require all of the same federal- and state-mandated tests as regular public schools because they are funded by public money. Given that many families leave the public school system to avoid testing, those who choose public charter schools have to decide if they are willing to participate in that same testing.

Parents who elect to take on the role of teacher in a highly structured homeschool setting experience more flexibility in tailoring selected curriculum to their child's unique situation (one of the biggest benefits of homeschooling), deciding what testing (if any) they want to do, and determining when they want their school day to start and which days they want to work. However, the trade-off for these families is the time involved in researching and selecting curriculum (an overwhelming process for many, given the extensive number of options), teaching, and then reviewing work, all of which requires a considerable commitment of both time and energy. Also, parents understand that the grades they assign on the child's final transcript, no matter how objective they try to be, may be considered less valid than those provided by an outside teacher or school.

Many families who prefer a structured approach elect to enroll in local community college classes as part of a dual enrollment program once their children are old enough. This option has the advantage of providing the structure they desire, in addition to providing formal grades and potential letters of recommendation for those applying to four-year institutions. Most families also recognize that this path helps prepare their student for the demands of higher education while demonstrating to admissions officers that their student is capable of doing college-level work, making this a very popular choice in the homeschooling community.

Little or No Structure: "Unschooling"

"Unschooling" is a term created and popularized by John Holt to describe an approach that recognizes and values the learner's choices and trusts his natural ability to learn outside of a classroom and without the "interference" of any adult. Other terms that describe this same approach include "life learning," "self-directed," or "child-led learning," but they all essentially boil down to the same conviction: learning happens all the time, in every situation, even without a curriculum. Adherents of unschooling believe that self-actualization through exploration of individual interests and passions in enriching environments is

> A child learns . . . not by using the procedure that seems best to us, but the one that seems best to him; by fitting into his structure of ideas and relationships, his mental model of reality, not the piece we think comes next, but the one he thinks comes next.
>
> ~John Holt, *How Children Fail*

what true learning is about, and parents who unschool their children trust that they will learn everything they need to learn without any of the conventions of schooling, like required subjects, assignments, and tests.

Even within the unschooling community, however, there is significant variation. On one end of the spectrum there are the most unstructured families, those who give their children complete freedom to direct their own learning without any requirements from the parents. At the other end, but still under the unschooling umbrella, are parents who see their role as providing a general level of guidance or encouragement related to learning, but still without setting any specific goals or tasks. In between are parents who function as guides or facilitators—supportive, but not directive.

Karin and her family are in the middle of the unschooling continuum, and are one of the families who felt comfortable enough to jump immediately in unschooling as soon they decided to pull their son, Jack, out of middle school. Like Max, whom we met earlier, school had never been easy for Jack. While he always had good relationships with his teachers and the other kids throughout elementary school, he struggled academically and required an individualized education program (IEP) every year, beginning in kindergarten. Karin and her husband became accustomed to working closely with Jack's teachers, supporting Jack in his school work at home, and attending the regular IEP meetings. As Karin says, "I had very traditional ideas of homeschooling, of a kid and parent sitting at the table doing schoolwork, and I didn't think it would be good for us." So, they did everything possible to work with the school system—homeschooling wasn't even on their radar.

The situation began to change in fifth grade. Around this time Jack began to experience bullying by some of his classmates, a situation that continued through middle school. Karin continued supporting her son at home and coordinating closely with his teachers and the principal, but at the beginning of eighth grade they hit a wall. Jack had become very anxious and stopped doing his homework, and one of his primary teachers began putting even more pressure on Jack to perform. His anxiety escalated further. As Karin reflects on that stressful time, she recalls, "I was just so tired of meetings and problems." So, she began reconsidering homeschooling as an option. After doing some reading and talking to other homeschooling families in her area, her family decided to try it. "I felt like I had jumped into the deep end of the pool, but I just knew traditional school was never going to work."

Jack's younger brother and sister remained in school as Jack and Karin embarked on their homeschooling journey. At first, Jack did not have much interest in doing academic things. Karin had discovered the idea of "deschooling" (taking time off to decompress after leaving school) in her initial research, so they took it easy, spending time working on a friend's farm, doing origami, and taking lessons at the music school.

Karin admits to having some anxiety as she worried about how she would cover all of the academic subjects with Jack and help him "keep up" with other kids his age, but her ongoing reading and expanding connections with other homeschoolers and unschoolers eased these concerns. And now that Jack has found some things he loves—bee keeping, music, wood working—she has been able to relax into their new lifestyle. In addition, Jack's younger brother, Finn, now unschools and loves it, as he pursues his interests in aeronautics and architecture.

Unschoolers tend to be quite satisfied and very positive about their lifestyle and tout its many benefits. In his 2013 research, "The Challenges and Benefits of Unschooling," which included a survey of over 200 unschooling families, Dr. Peter Gray found that:

The reported benefits of unschooling were numerous; they included improved learning, better attitudes about learning, and improved psychological and social well-being for the children; and increased closeness, harmony, and freedom for the whole family.[1]

These families reported some challenges too, though, most notably "that of overcoming feelings of criticism, or social pressure, that came from others who disapproved and from their own culturally-ingrained, habitual ways of thinking about education."[2] In short, living at the far end of the continuum, furthest from traditional and familiar educational approaches, has significant benefits, but also leaves some families feeling separate from the majority, and often even separate from other homeschoolers.

It is almost impossible to know how many students are unschooled out of the millions who are homeschooled. However, in his same research, Peter Gray reports that:

> [B]ased on their prevalence at homeschooling conventions and estimates from people familiar with homeschooling generally, our best guess is that roughly ten percent of homeschoolers would identify themselves as unschoolers, and that percentage seems to be growing over time.

If this is an accurate estimate, this means that there are currently approximately 250,000 unschoolers in the United States, with more joining this community every year.

Some Structure: "Eclectic"

Eclectic homeschoolers are in the middle of the spectrum, incorporating aspects of both the structured educational approach and unstructured learning. Eclectic homeschooling can best be described as a unique mix of styles and methods selected to best meet the needs, interests, and learning preferences of the student, while also integrating specific educational goals that are often chosen by the parents. Many eclectic homeschoolers choose a more structured approach for subjects like math, science, and writing, and then give their children more freedom to choose the types of books they want to read and other special interests and activities they want to pursue. Cooperatives and unit studies, topical lessons and projects that cross multiple subjects, are frequently incorporated in the regular routines of many eclectic homeschoolers to provide their children with exposure to other adults who supply expertise in certain subjects and to integrate learning. Many eclectic homeschoolers also take advantage of the opportunity to attend a few select classes at their local school.

Wendy and her husband have opted for an eclectic approach to their children's education, and have homeschooled their three sons, now ages sixteen, fourteen, and twelve, since the beginning. Her husband was the first to mention the idea of homeschooling before their first son was even school-aged, but Wendy, a music and theater teacher, was initially against it. "I told him, 'No, homeschoolers are weird.'" Plus, Wendy had taught several homeschooled students as they were transitioning back into public school and knew it had not been easy for them—she did not want her children to be in the same position someday.

So, when her first son was old enough, they enrolled him in pre-school, but right from the beginning it did not go well. Wendy says of that experience, "He cried every day, even though the teacher was good and all the other kids loved her." Separating every day was upsetting to him, and Wendy agreed that it was not working for her either. She began to reconsider homeschooling, and the next year she left her job to stay home with her son.

Over a decade later, and now with three boys, this choice has definitely worked well for their family. It did take some time for them to find the approach that worked best for them, though. At the beginning they tried a more structured approach, using the Classical Model of education, but "everyone was too stressed," so they reconsidered. What they ultimately decided to do, and have been doing for several years now, is a structured curriculum for math, science, and writing (the boys get to choose their own topics) four days a week, with the boys free to pursue other interests the rest of the time. Interestingly, all three boys have chosen to attend their local public schools part-time, taking elective classes in band, choir, and theater.

One of the highlights of their homeschooling experience so far has been a three-month road trip Wendy and the boys took up the east coast of the United States (her husband joining when he could), beginning in Key West and ending in Maine. The purpose of the trip was to study US history, and they stopped and toured many Civil War and Revolutionary War battlefields along the way. Having grown up on the west coast, the boys were also quite taken with the historic architecture of the east coast, and Wendy says that seeing the actual places where the events they had read about took place had a big impact on them as well—it was a "learning experience they'll never forget."

The boys have always had the option to go to school full-time, but have never been interested. The benefits that come along with this lifestyle seem to be appreciated by everyone in the family. Both Wendy and her husband have a close connection with each of the boys, which Wendy attributes to the lack of negative outside influences, "even though the boys have a good amount of independence and their own activities," and the brothers have close relationships with each other. This does not mean that they have not had any concerns or worries. Now that the older two are starting to think about college, Wendy is beginning to wonder if she has done enough to prepare them academically and to help them develop skills like time management and workload management— common concerns among homeschooling parents.

Crossing Categories: World Schooling

Now that we have explored both the ends and middle of the homeschooling continuum, we are going to add a twist. Remember, the one rule of homeschooling is that there are no hard and fast delineations between motivations, demographics, or educational philosophies— homeschoolers rarely fit neatly to any one category, which could not be truer for any type of homeschooler than it is for "world schoolers." The briefest way to describe world schooling is "an educational approach that emphasizes learning from the world." Most families who have chosen this lifestyle travel *a lot*. Some have home bases from which they launch their travelling, often for a few weeks or months at a time, returning regularly to plan their next adventure. Others are more nomadic, spending a few months or years in one location, before picking up and moving on to the next.

> **The reasons we world school**
>
> 1. We love to travel.
> 2. Walking on glaciers teaches more than reading about one and visiting CERN is a great way to learn about particle physics.
> 3. Meeting people and learning cultures and languages is simple when you get up and go.
>
> ~Carolyn, world schooling mother of two

The majority of world schoolers seem to describe their educational approach as mostly unstructured, taking advantage of whatever their location offers. Whether it is archeological explorations and the history (not to mention languages) of their current country, or marine biology and nature studies of a new environment, world schoolers truly embrace "learning from the world." Some, however, also describe a more structured approach to education, identifying as either "eclectic," incorporating some sort of planned lessons or activities into a typical day, or even "traditional," enrolling in local schools for part of the time they reside in an area.

Mickelle and her husband chose this option for their two children, ten and seven years old. Before embarking on their world schooling adventure, their daughter attended a Montessori preschool, then a charter school through second grade, and their son attended preschool. When they arrived in Guatemala, their first world schooling location, Mickelle enrolled the kids in an international school where she also taught a third/fourth grade class. Since then, they have lived in six countries over a two-year span, and have shifted to a more eclectic style.

Mickelle says they do not really have a typical day, and describes their current approach as having little structure. They have elementary-level supplementary math materials that they use when they can, usually completing a lesson or two a day, and they have subscribed to a reading curriculum that allows them to download books from the library. As Mickelle summarizes, "I feel like my kids are growing daily as readers, and I'm not having to do anything to help." Otherwise, Mickelle follows the kids' lead, providing "activities that I believe are appropriate and fun for them." Science and social studies activities often happen naturally, depending on what opportunities emerge from their current location and the interests and questions her kids express.

Many people outside of the homeschooling community find it surprising when they meet a parent like Mickelle, with a background in education, who has decided to withdraw their children from the system. In fact, Mickelle is not uncommon—many former teachers and administrators choose to homeschool (including Wendy, whom we met earlier). Why would people who obviously value education, and who have invested time and money in licenses and credentials that enable them to teach, abandon the system they had once worked so hard to be a part of? Mickelle explains her decision this way:

> *There's too much wasted time in school and too much emphasis on the wrong ideas—traditional, segregated subjects, grades, and formal assessments. As a National Board Certified Teacher, I learned to always ask, "What is the impact on student learning?" Too often, I was unsatisfied with the answers. In addition to this, I've read studies concluding that the retention rates for the curriculum students learn in schools are low. I knew I could do better.*

The challenges of this lifestyle are somewhat different than most homeschoolers experience. World schoolers frequently find the lack of access to materials or extra-curricular activities in other countries frustrating. The same with figuring out the complex problem of making a living while on the road. In addition, language barriers and regularly saying good-bye to new friends are difficult. The benefits of world schooling are not hard to imagine, though, as they include many of the same benefits other homeschoolers experience, augmented by unique cross-cultural experiences.

Crossing Categories: Democratic Schools

Students who attend democratic schools are not usually counted as homeschoolers, but I include them here because they face many of the same challenges as homeschoolers in the college application process in that they generally do not have standard transcripts, grades, or high school course sequences. In fact, some people refer to democratic schools as "unschooling schools," because they offer students a completely self-directed learning experience within a community that grants them full responsibility for making decisions about their lives and learning. As members of this community, all students and adults (who serve as guides and facilitators) discuss and vote together on issues that affect the community, including which classes will be offered (if any), who can join the school, and which rules they want the members of the community to abide by as they play and work together.

Those who are skeptical about home education and question its effectiveness generally hold the same concerns about democratic schools, wondering how younger children and teens could possibly make responsible decisions about their education without any external requirements. Given that some democratic schools have been around for decades, we can easily find information about how their graduates have fared after they leave and as they enter adulthood. Several studies of the graduates of one of the more well-known democratic schools, Sudbury Valley School in Massachusetts, have been conducted over time, one of which was conducted by Boston College and published in the *American Journal of Education*. In short, the authors of this study concluded that:

> *Although these children educated themselves in ways that are enormously different from what occurs at traditional schools, they have no apparent difficulty being admitted to or adjusting to the demands of traditional higher education and have been successful in a wide variety of careers.* [3]

Other well-known democratic schools include Summerhill in England and the Fairhaven School in Maryland. Two principal organizations supporting alternative education and the values that democratic schools like these promote are the Institute for Democratic Education in America (IDEA) and the Alternative Education Resource Organization (AERO), both of which serve as sources of information for parents, teachers, and schools through their websites, books, articles, and national and regional conferences.

Conclusion

As we have seen in the stories of homeschooling in these first two chapters, most families do not take the homeschooling lifestyle lightly. Those who choose alternative forms of education report strong feelings of anxiety as they break away from an established and familiar system, inform family and friends who do not always understand or support this choice, and navigate the vagueness and uncertainty of the benefits through the first months. In addition, the lifestyle requires certain trade-offs that affect the entire family, often including one parent putting her own professional life on hold (or at least slowing it down), and shifting to a more "learning-oriented" mindset in their daily lives as regular lessons and activities are planned and managed. In short, pursuing homeschooling and other alternative forms of education is not easy. Additionally, several widely-held myths persist about homeschoolers which those in this community encounter regularly, often putting them in the position of defending their choice to others. Let us take a closer look at some of the most common misconceptions, and explore which may hold some elements of truth.

Chapter Three

The Four Most Common Misconceptions of Homeschoolers

Peter Gray's research focusing on unschoolers (mentioned in Chapter Two) suggests that one of the most difficult aspects of unschooling is dealing with the outside opinions and criticisms of this choice. Most homeschoolers, not just unschoolers, face this challenge as family, friends, new acquaintances, and even strangers express their views and pose questions to parents who have chosen to raise and educate their children differently. Concern about a child's welfare and lack of understanding about homeschooling are usually the source of people's well-intentioned inquiries, which seem to center on four main issues:

1. Homeschooled children are unsocialized.
2. Homeschoolers are religious.
3. Only wealthy families can homeschool.
4. Parents cannot teach better than a licensed teacher.

Misconception #1: Homeschooled Children Are Unsocialized

Though the majority of homeschoolers have been confronted with one or more of the four beliefs listed above at one time or another, the idea of the "unsocialized homeschooler" is especially wide-spread and pernicious, and is the cause of a fair amount of eye-rolling among homeschooling parents. In fact, if you want to trigger a lively conversation among a group of homeschooling parents, just ask them how many times they have been asked the "socialization question."

Many people believe that homeschoolers are overly sheltered from their peers and community, with the common image of homeschoolers sitting at the kitchen table doing schoolwork. Yet, as described previously, most homeschoolers spend a significant portion of

> *There seems to be an overwhelming amount of evidence that children socialized in a peer-dominant environment are at higher risk for developing social maladjustment issues than those [who] are socialized in a parent-monitored environment.*
>
> ~Michael S. Brady, Psychologist

their time away from home, taking advantage of multiple learning opportunities like attending art classes, joining science clubs, organizing trips to museums and historical sites, meeting with tutors and mentors, volunteering, traveling, participating in co-ops, and regularly interacting with people of all ages and backgrounds in their communities. In fact, because of these varied experiences that include other people from a wide range of backgrounds and ages, many homeschooling families argue that their kids are better socialized than those who are restricted to age-grouped classes in school for most of the day.

This idea that homeschooled students are at least as well, and possibly better, socialized than their publicly- and privately-schooled peers is supported by a review of research conducted by psychology professor Richard Medlin. In his 2013 report, "Homeschooling and the Question of Socialization Revisited," published in the *Peabody Journal of Education*, he summarizes his conclusions this way:

> *The research indicates that homeschooling parents expect their children to respect and get along with people of diverse backgrounds, provide their children with a variety of social opportunities outside the family, and believe their children's social skills are at least as good as those of other children. Compared to children attending conventional schools, research suggests that they have higher quality friendships and better relationships with their parents and other adults. They are happy, optimistic, and satisfied with their lives. Their moral reasoning is at least as advanced as that of other children, and they may be more likely to act unselfishly. As adolescents, they have a strong sense of social responsibility and exhibit less emotional turmoil and problem behaviors than their peers. Those who go on to college are socially involved and open to new experiences. Adults who were homeschooled as children are civically engaged and functioning competently in every way measured so far. An alarmist view of homeschooling, therefore, is not supported by empirical research.*[1]

So, it would seem that there is little cause for concern on this issue. And as homeschooled children grow into adolescence and young adulthood, rather than developing into insecure social misfits, they demonstrate themselves to be quite socially competent and capable of sustaining close relationships and engaging in their community. In addition, one of the many reasons parents frequently choose to homeschool is because of socialization issues, like the peer pressure and bullying their children have encountered in traditional schools.

But how do homeschooled students themselves feel about this, particularly teens, for whom having friends and an active social life is so important? In her survey of homeschoolers mentioned earlier, Sue Patterson asked homeschooled teens the question, "Did you find enough friends?" Eighty-five percent of those who responded said they were "satisfied with the number of friends" they had. As Sue explains, "They, often with their parents' help, found an enormous array of options for meeting other teenagers and experiencing a full and rich social life."[2] Kirby, a grown homeschooler who participated in the project, reported, "I met tons and tons of people, but it was not just teenagers. I prided myself for having a variety of ages within my several circles of friends."

Having friends is not the only important aspect of socialization. Socialization also includes the ability to work with a team, follow the lead of an instructor or boss, and generally get along with diverse groups of people. For those in higher education, these types of social skills are the most relevant to consider given that success in college (and in the working world beyond) requires the ability to participate within a classroom or workplace setting, and effectively operate within and contribute to teams. It is this aspect of socialization that gives some admissions officers a certain amount of concern. In the 2004 report, "A Study of Admissions Officers' Perceptions of and Attitudes Toward

Homeschool Students," the authors found that, although a significant majority of admissions officers expected homeschooled students to do as well or better academically than traditional students, "almost thirty-five percent expected homeschooled graduates would not cope as well as traditional high school graduates."[3] This finding is consistent with my own more recent research (which I will describe in more detail in the next chapter), and underscores the fact that the assumption of lack of socialization is still a hurdle that many homeschoolers must continue to overcome, despite substantial evidence and numerous examples to the contrary.

> In the public school system, children are socialized horizontally, and temporarily, into conformity to their immediate peers. Home educators seek to socialize their children vertically, towards responsibility, service, and adulthood, with an eye on eternity.
>
> ~Thomas Smedley,
> "Socialization of Homeschool Children, A Communication Approach"

Misconception #2: Homeschoolers are Religious

The misconception is not that homeschoolers are religious, but rather that *all* homeschoolers are religious. While it is true that the number of homeschooling parents who choose to incorporate religious instruction in their children's education is still a majority of the homeschooling population, it is also true that secular homeschooling represents a significant and quickly growing portion of the community. Once again, however, given how difficult it is to study a population as distributed and varied as homeschoolers, it is tough to know for sure exactly how many secular homeschoolers there are, or even what the ratio of religious to non-religious homeschooling families might be.

Given that the NCES data discussed earlier indicates that sixty-four percent of homeschooling families have indicated that providing religious instruction is an "important" reason for homeschooling, we might estimate that roughly two-thirds of homeschoolers are religious, and one-third are secular.

Two reasons seem to account for the rapid growth of the secular homeschooling numbers:

1. Growing dissatisfaction with academic instruction at public schools
2. An increase in the number of people who identify as atheist or agnostic

As discussed earlier, as of 2012, two of the top three reasons parents gave as their primary motive for homeschooling related to the environment and quality of academic instruction in schools—not religion. This is a change from NCES surveys in the years prior to 2012, which consistently reported that the "desire to provide religious instruction" was the chief reason parents chose to homeschool. In light of this change, we can assume that the level of dissatisfaction with the public education system has reached a point which motivates a higher proportion of secular families to join the homeschooling movement. In addition, technology is enabling easier access to secular educational resources, content, and support groups, making it simpler for non-religious families to find the types of materials and support they desire—an important development given how dominant Christian-based curriculum and materials have been.

The second likely factor is that more Americans now identify as atheist or agnostic. According to the Pew Research Center, "the percentage of Americans who are religiously unaffiliated—describing themselves as atheist, agnostic or 'nothing in particular'—has jumped more than six points, from 16.1 percent to 22.8 percent" from 2007 to 2014, especially among those under age fifty.[4] Since parents of school-aged children generally fall into this age group, a larger percentage of this population identifying as "non-religious" would result in a larger percentage of homeschoolers identifying as non-religious. In short, the increase in secular homeschoolers is likely, at least in part, to be a reflection of the increase of secular adults in the general population.

Secular homeschooling families are obviously not afraid to opt out of dominant cultural institutions like religious institutions and the public-school system, which means they continue to represent a small subsection of American culture. So, what else do we know about these families? According to the same Pew research, non-religiously affiliated adults tend to be politically liberal (sixty-nine percent) and highly educated (forty-three percent have a college degree compared to twenty-seven percent of the general population). Certainly many adults who are members of religious organizations also describe themselves as "liberal" and "highly educated," so these descriptors are not limited to secular adults. However, it seems that secular homeschoolers are more likely to hold liberal views and to have attended college, which means that these are other criteria that may set them apart from the current majority.

As for the homeschooling families who do identify as members of a religious group, it is important to note that, even for Christian families, "providing religious instruction" is not always their primary reason for homeschooling, nor is it always the focus of the educational approach they select. Therefore, concerns about the quality and inclusiveness of the education these students have achieved, most notably in the subject of science, need to be recognized and questioned. Those who want to understand current demographics and trends within the homeschooling community need to keep in mind that making assumptions about what it means to be a homeschooler, particularly with respect to their educational philosophy and potential limitations, may not true for a large portion of this population.

Misconception #3: Only Wealthy Families Can Homeschool

This third misconception comes from the idea that, in order to homeschool, one parent must stay home to teach the children while the other parent earns enough to support the family on a single income. While in many homeschooling families one of the parents does not have a full-time job outside of the home, in a significant number of families the parent primarily responsible for homeschooling does have a job— sometimes full-time, sometimes part-time, and often with the flexibility to work from home. In fact, many homeschooling parents talk about how they have had to be creative in arranging their work life (e.g., one parent works a night or swing shift while the other works traditional hours) and to make some hard choices about priorities in terms of family finances (e.g., moving to smaller homes or reducing their living expenses in other ways in order to make this lifestyle possible).

But are these families wealthy? Some of the most recent research reports that homeschooling families are wealthier than average, but much of this research has relied on volunteer participants completing their surveys, not necessarily a random sample of homeschoolers, so it is therefore highly unlikely that these survey results are representative of the general homeschooling population. The more reliable, and likely more representative, data comes from the National Center for Education Statistics (NCES) study,[5] which drew from a large random sample and asked questions about education in general, not just homeschooling specifically. This data suggests that the income of homeschooling families actually mirrors the income of the general population fairly closely, and that homeschooling families are just as likely to be poor as other families in the United States. The homeschooling community is comprised of families from all income levels, including two-income families, single-income families, and even single-parent families.

But how do working parents manage to homeschool their children while also coping with typical job responsibilities? In an article for *Fast Company*, Laura Vanderkam summarized some of the strategies that working/homeschooling families use to "build a career while running a small school operation at the same time."[6] A key step in creating and managing this lifestyle? Do the math. As Vanderkam learned, "You can work forty hours and homeschool for twenty hours, sleep eight hours a night (fifty-six per week), and still have fifty-two hours for other things. The key is moving the pieces around." Between local homeschooling programs and co-ops, tutors, sitters, the other parent, and extended family, many families who would laugh at the idea of being described as "wealthy" have managed to successfully put the pieces in place.

Misconception #4: Parents Cannot Teach Better Than a Licensed Teacher

Like the question of socialization, this perception persists because it has a strong ring of truth to it—teachers train for years to get their teaching license, so how could a parent possibly hope to teach her children without similar preparation? And even for those who allow that maybe a parent could effectively homeschool her children through elementary school (when basic reading, writing, and math are all that are required), once those children reach junior high and high school and need to learn more complicated material like trigonometry and chemistry, how can one parent be qualified to teach all these advanced subjects?

To address this particular issue, we can begin by taking a look at the average academic results of homeschoolers. According to Dr. Brian Ray of the National Home Education Research Institute (NHERI), "The home-educated typically score fifteen to thirty percentile points above public-school students on standardized academic achievement tests."[7] He goes on to report, "Homeschool students score above average on achievement tests regardless of their parents' level of formal education or their family's household income." These results are consistent across multiple tests of academic ability that compare homeschoolers to traditionally-educated students. So, somehow these students who have been educated at home are managing to "keep up" academically. But how?

It comes back to the many resources and approaches available: tutors, online courses, printed curriculum and materials, co-ops, and community college classes, just to name a few. Homeschoolers take advantage of a wide variety of sources of information and learn how to find "teachers," in whatever form or location they may exist, outside of traditional schools. Also, note that for the vast majority of homeschooling families, especially those with older students, the parents primarily take on a facilitator or coaching role, not a teaching role. If we could do an activity analysis and see how average homeschooling parents spend their school-related time, regardless of their approach to homeschooling and where they are on the structure continuum, it would very likely look something like the graph below, "Estimated Activity Categories for Homeschooling Parents." In short, parents of younger students tend to spend more time every day directly teaching or guiding, with some facilitation time as they connect their students with outside opportunities like art classes, while parents of older students spend increasingly more time helping their students find and connect with non-

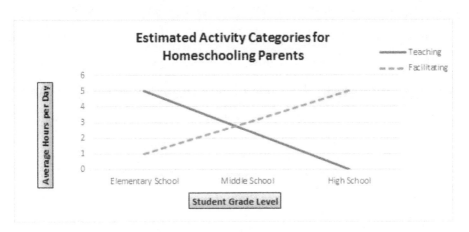

parent learning options, which frequently include online classes or community college classes, jobs and internships, tutors, and mentors. So, parents do not need to be able to teach, and many do not even see teaching as their primary role. Instead, they spend the majority of their time connecting, guiding, and facilitating, with positive results.

Parental level of education may also affect the academic success of homeschoolers. As shown in the NCES data provided earlier, approximately forty percent of parents who choose to educate their children at home also have a college degree. These parents are frequently mothers who have cut back their working hours or put their careers on hold, and who place a high level of importance on education and set high standards for their children. The results of Dr. Brian Ray's previously mentioned 2010 nationwide study of homeschoolers confirmed the positive correlation that parental levels of higher education have with homeschooling outcomes, reporting that "homeschool children whose parents are both college graduates outperform children whose parents both do not have a college degree."[8] Still, as the author points out, "parents' education level explains only 2.5 percent of the variance in the scores." Ray also concluded that even in families where neither parent holds a college degree, the average test results of the homeschooled students are still higher than those of students in public schools. Finally, and most surprisingly, this study found that the students whose parents had never held a teaching certification scored higher than those who did have at least one parent who was or had been a certified teacher.

So, overall it appears that homeschoolers perform academically at least as well as, and often better than, their public-school peers, likely due to the high value that homeschooling families place on education, regardless of their parents' educational status or attainment of a teaching credential, in addition to the focused and personal attention that these students receive, and a broad access to all types of educational resources.

Other Misconceptions

Other common misconceptions of homeschoolers revolve around studying-related skills, including lack of time management skills and inexperience with doing the "hard things" in life, like getting up early every day to go to classes or work. While it might be true that homeschoolers who have experienced a less structured form of education, like unschoolers, may not have as much practice working with deadlines for submitting papers or other school projects, it is also true that it does not take twelve years to learn how to set an alarm or develop a study schedule. And it is the rare student, even among the least-structured homeschoolers, who has not participated on some sort of team or group activity that required regular practices or meetings, games or presentations.

The role of motivation is important here, too. Most adults know how different it feels to plan and participate in something that interests them versus something they "have" to do. Home educated students are no different—not only are they able to work on rigorous or challenging projects requiring persistence and "grit," but they also have the experience of feeling ownership of the results, including their own learning. In short, they know what it is like to be self-driven and, especially by the time they reach high school age, understand how to handle the specifics of their own education. Any small gaps in their experience upon arriving on a college campus or into the working world are usually minor and easily resolved, as we will see in Chapter Six.

Conclusion

Clearly, school just does not work for everyone, and an increasing number of parents see homeschooling as the best option for helping kids develop to their fullest academic, social, and creative potential. As one gifted homeschooled student explained, "The best part about going to school was the social part, feeling like a 'normal' kid. But I just did not get much out of it academically. I was really bored. It just started to feel like a big waste of time."

And yet, many of these students say they are very interested in attending college, reporting that higher education aligns with their professional interests and personal goals. When the time comes to apply, however, many face unexpected expectations and hurdles, even when they are academically equipped and feel they have planned and prepared sufficiently. So where do the gaps appear between these highly-motivated students and the higher education community?

Chapter Four

A National Survey of Homeschoolers and Admissions Officers

In 2014, when the older of my two sons began eighth grade, we started discussing and planning what he wanted to do for high school. Did he want to try attending a regular high school, or did he want to continue homeschooling? Did he prefer a more structured approach to learning, or a more flexible one? An important part of the conversation included college planning, because we knew that the homeschooling approach we selected would determine which choices would be available to him in four years. Was he interested in going to college? If so, did he already have an idea of what he wanted to study? If not, what other options did he want to consider? While we did not come up with any final decisions at the time, we continue to revisit these questions, especially now that we are homeschooling him through high school, and new options and ideas surface each time we talk about it. What has remained consistent throughout our conversations is that college is definitely on his radar—all the career paths that interest him require at least an undergraduate degree. So, back in eighth grade, I added "college counselor" to my list of homeschooling roles, and began researching college admissions for homeschoolers.

Amid the abundant information and advice available online about creating high school transcripts and deciding which exams to take, I came across a 2004 study published by the *Journal of College Admission* and conducted by Dr. Paul Jones and Dr. Gene Gloeckner entitled, "A Study of Admissions Officers' Perceptions of and Attitudes toward Homeschool Students." The title grabbed me immediately, hitting right at the heart of my apprehension—not just the tactical aspects of the college application process, but how my son's application would be viewed when unknown admissions readers pulled his file out of the stack, opened it up, and saw "homeschooled." I cannot help but think back to my days on the MBA program's admissions committee, and how critically I viewed the files of our non-traditional applicants. Are they academically qualified? Will they add anything to our program? Now on the other side of the process, I have been deeply concerned about the exact issue this 2004 study examined: "The attitudes and perceptions of college admission personnel toward the homeschooled graduate."

Fortunately, the findings of the study were unexpectedly reassuring. According to the authors:

> *Overall, the attitudes and perceptions of admission officers were favorable toward the expected success of the homeschooled graduate. More than seventy-three percent of the admission officers anticipated that homeschooled graduates would be as successful or more successful in their first-year of college.*[1]

So, academically, homeschooled students seem to be on a level playing field with other applicants, at least as far as perceptions are concerned. Regarding social adjustment, however, the study also found that thirty-five percent of colleges and universities expected homeschooled applicants would not "cope socially as well as their traditional school peers," and further, that many of these schools were, at least back in 2004, "reluctant to change their personal interview policies" for homeschoolers. So, some misconceptions and barriers still existed, but that was ten years prior to the time I was doing my own investigation. Given the rapid growth of the homeschooling population, and presumably the growth of the number of homeschooled students who have applied and been accepted to college in the intervening decade, I wanted to know if these perceptions had changed. So in 2015 I decided to launch my own survey of admissions officers to update our understanding of current trends and issues by re-asking many of the same questions included in Jones and Gloeckner's research. I also wanted to ensure that the survey addressed current homeschoolers' issues and concerns, so I decided to begin with a national survey of homeschoolers, asking them about their college-related priorities and questions. The results were quite interesting.

Research Part 1
From Home Education to Higher Education:
What Homeschoolers Want to Know

With the support of the Oregon Home Education Network (OHEN), the primary homeschooling support organization in my state, I designed and launched the online survey "From Home Education to

Higher Education: What Homeschoolers Want to Know" at the beginning of 2015. After publishing several articles about our research on national homeschooling websites and publications, which invited homeschooling parents across the country to share their experiences and concerns with us, I also contacted homeschooling organizations in other states via email, asking them to invite their member families to participate. Over the course of the next few months, we received almost 150 responses from homeschoolers in every region of the country, with the most responses from the Pacific states (Washington, Oregon, California, Alaska, and Hawaii). Almost fifty percent of the respondents reported that they were experienced homeschoolers, having homeschooled for more than five years and, more interesting, approximately ninety percent indicated that their child was "extremely likely" or "very likely" to attend college. So, while the responses we received do not necessarily represent a random sampling of all homeschoolers, the issues and concerns that parents expressed through the survey are likely representative of most college-bound homeschoolers.

After the survey's demographic questions, the first two multiple-choice questions asked which issues related to college admissions for homeschoolers are most important, and how the process could be made easier. In response to the first question, "understanding the documentation required" and "understanding test requirements" were both ranked as "highly important" by more than eighty percent of the respondents. Of least importance was the issue of "understanding the application process" (including steps and key dates). So, it appears that while most parents are fairly comfortable with the general process and deadlines, they are still not certain which documents and tests are required for homeschooled students. As one parent inquired in the comments section, "I need to understand how tests are changing due to Common Core and how that affects those of us who are not using CC curriculum. Is there a specific test we should or should not take?" In terms of what would make the admissions process easier for homeschooled students, eighty percent of respondents indicated that "a dedicated page on the college website for homeschoolers" would be helpful, and over seventy percent responded that both "a sample homeschool transcript" and "a checklist for the application process" would be valuable. Surprisingly, the least-selected options for this question were "a dedicated liaison or counselor" and "admissions workshops for homeschoolers," although more than half of respondents still indicated that these would be appreciated, and many of the comments included requests for these types of support as well.

Parents also posed additional (and very specific) concerns and requests to the two subsequent open-ended questions. The first of these was the question, "If there were one thing you would like admissions officers to know about homeschooled students, what would it be?" This question received more responses than any of the other open-response questions in the survey by far, with

> We believe in whole learning and [that] grades are not an indication of learning achieved. Help us help you translate that into terms you can understand.
>
> ~Homeschooling Parent

over seventy percent of the survey participants providing an answer (the average response rate for the other open-response questions was closer to fifty percent). General themes that emerged from these responses include the assertions that homeschooled students are "different but still qualified," that they are often above average in both academics and maturity, and that they have high levels of motivation for learning and are largely independent and self-directed learners. Another observation about the responses to this question is that many included a defensive tone, assuming a bias against homeschooled students both in terms of their academic achievements and college readiness, as well as their socialization skills (the "socialization question" mentioned in the prior chapter). Several of these referred to interactions that had already taken place with college personnel, so some of the defensiveness seemed to be based on direct experience. A final theme that clearly emerged in the response set to this question related to additional and unfair requirements for homeschoolers, or "extra hoops" they need to clear, compared to traditional students.

Finally, when given the opportunity to "ask an admissions officer any question," the desire for more information and more specific guidance clearly came through in almost every comment. Sample questions ranged from general requests such as, "How can we best communicate our academic experience, knowledge and life lessons so that you can apply them to your entrance requirements?" to more specific appeals like, "What do you see in homeschool students that you value?" In addition, parents are seeking information and support not only related to the application process, but also about perceptions, recommendations, and insights of college personnel. The desire to understand the needs, interests, and advice of those on the admissions side of the process in order to more effectively "help you help us" was reflected in the majority of questions posed. (For additional responses on this and the prior survey questions discussed, see Appendix A.)

Undoubtedly, the parents we heard from are searching for the best methods to advocate for their children and communicate their varied and unique learning experiences to people on the college side who do not know them, whom they fear may not understand or appreciate their students' accomplishments. Many seem particularly frustrated by the need to document their child's educational activities and qualifications on standard forms like the Common Application that were created for a different type of student, and by the lack of direct access to someone on the other side of the process who can answer questions and provide specific guidance.

With homeschooling families on one shore and higher education administrators and faculty on the other, the current shaky "information bridge" connecting them could use some additional support. While some parents acknowledge that the general information already provided for homeschooled applicants on admissions websites is helpful, their comments indicate that they would like to have even more specific information, more clear-cut examples and guidelines of what admissions officers and committees are looking for in terms of transcript format and content, testing options, transfer credit, scholarship eligibility, and a general sense that homeschoolers are welcome at the institution. Further, homeschoolers would find it helpful to understand during the college planning period which college-specific supplements and supplemental evaluations (from employers, coaches, or volunteer supervisors) the college will accept as part of the Common Application.

So, this is the view of college admissions from the homeschooling shore. The concerns, requests, and questions posed by these families helped inform the next phase of this research, a survey of admissions officers and other higher education personnel standing on the other shore.

Research Part II
From Home Education to Higher Education:
A Study of Admissions' Officers Perceptions of
Homeschooled Students

Based on what we learned from representative homeschooling families across the country, along with the model of the research conducted by Jones and Gloeckner in 2004, several board members from the Oregon Home Education Network (OHEN) helped me design and test a survey that was distributed to admissions officers across the country in the spring of 2015 via email invitation and a link to our online version of the survey. We incorporated many of the same questions included in the 2004 research, along with a few additional questions of our own. As with the initial survey of homeschoolers, we began collecting responses fairly quickly. Overall, fifty-eight admissions professionals, including vice presidents of enrollment, assistant deans of admission, and directors/assistant directors of admissions, along with a few faculty members, responded to the twenty-four questions in the survey (most of which were multiple choice, but many of which included options for comments). Once again, we heard from people across the country representing schools of all sizes and types, including several

74

highly selective schools, numerous public universities, and multiple smaller liberal arts schools.

In both the email invitation and the written introduction to the survey, anonymity was promised to all research respondents, assuring them that neither their participation nor their specific responses would be shared. My thinking in making this promise to the participants was that people would be more likely to share any negative perceptions or personal reservations under these conditions, information that could be useful to homeschoolers. Further supporting this choice was the fact that I was interested in gaining and sharing information about general perceptions and policies, not those of any one school. However, as I began poring over the initial responses in the fall of 2015, I realized that many homeschoolers might be interested in knowing how different schools responded and, as I write this book, I know it would be helpful to share particular practices, application and admission rates, and helpful insights with other schools who may be reviewing and updating their application process and admissions policies for homeschoolers. Unfortunately, it is too late to change the deal with the survey participants now, but I am happy to report that the final array of findings and insights should be truly helpful to everyone interested and involved in college admissions for homeschoolers, including counselors, college-side admissions professionals, and homeschooling families. Additionally, I contacted many of the schools who participated in the survey, especially those that seem to have some interesting admissions policies, processes and perspectives, and I will be sharing this "best practices" information in Chapter Six.

The admissions professionals who participated in our 2015 survey turned out to be quite an experienced group. One-third reported that they have been working in admissions anywhere between four and ten years, and forty-four percent have worked in admissions for over ten years. In addition, admissions work is the primary role for eighty-nine percent of the respondents (spending seventy-five to one hundred percent of their work time in this capacity), while it is only a part-time role for the remainder of those who responded. The survey group represents colleges and universities of all types and sizes, but the majority of them are from private institutions (sixty-four percent), and a large percentage have 5,000 or fewer students on campus (seventy-right percent). However, several state universities and church-affiliated admissions officers also participated, as did admissions officers from larger schools, eleven percent of which have more than 10,000 students on campus. Rural, suburban, and urban campus settings were evenly represented, and all but one respondent indicated that their school accepts homeschooled applicants. As for official homeschool admission policies, well over half reported that their school does have such a policy, while about a third indicated that their school does not (with the remainder indicating they were not sure).

The next section of the survey included several questions about the specific documents either required or recommended in the admissions process for homeschoolers, along with their level of importance. Further, an option to include additional details or clarifications in the comments section was provided, and a quarter to a third of our survey respondents chose to provide this additional information on several questions. It is not surprising that the most important of the required documents for virtually all of the schools participating in this survey are academic transcripts and standardized admissions test scores. Based on the comments provided, however, the type of transcripts that different schools accept vary, with some indicating that they need "proof of an accredited curriculum and transcript through an area or state educational authority," while others are open to narrative transcripts with "no set format," as long as they "provide detail of the subjects that students have covered during their homeschool years."

Third and fourth on the list of required admissions documents were essays and letters of recommendation, with multiple respondents sharing the advice that, "Letters of recommendation cannot be from a family member. They must be from someone else who knows the student such as an outside tutor or an employer." Surprisingly, a GED, SAT subject tests, and personal interviews were ranked quite low in level of importance, and are not required

> If the student has taken a really "traditional" type of homeschool curriculum and won't have a traditional high school transcript then we rely more on standardized testing . . . so, in this instance SAT Subject or AP Exams may help improve their application.
>
> ~Director of Admissions

by most schools for homeschooled applicants. Yet, when asked about recommended materials (versus required materials), subject tests and interviews were frequently mentioned, including the advice to "take more than two SAT subject tests," and the guidance that, "Interviews are recommended for all students, and are often particularly advantageous for homeschooled students." Other optional materials recommended by some admissions officers include a resume, in-person portfolio reviews, and "any additional documents that may give us a better sense of the student's academic abilities." One admissions director further advised homeschooled students to "use the 'additional information' section on the common application to address the question of how you can show what you know and why you chose the path you did. Always do the optional parts of the app—it can only help you!"

The next set of questions asked about the number of applications each school received from homeschooled students in the most recent academic year, and how this number compares to prior years. The largest percentage of schools reported that they received between eleven and twenty-nine applications, while about a third said that they received between thirty and forty-nine. Approximately fourteen percent reported that they received more than forty-nine applications from homeschoolers, with one admissions officer noting in the comments section that their school received sixty applications from homeschoolers out of a total of 15,000. The survey did not ask what percentage of total applications this number represents (which is a question that will be added in future versions of the survey), but it is safe to assume that applications from homeschooled applicants still represent a fairly small percentage of overall applications. Given that almost 14,000 homeschooled students took the SAT in 2014, however, the number of applications from this group across all colleges and universities is still considerable, and appears to be growing, with one hundred percent of our survey respondents indicating that the number of applications they have received from homeschoolers in recent years is either "about the same" or "increasing."

Next, we asked admissions officers to tell us about their expectations of how well homeschoolers would perform in their first year of college as measured by grade point average, retention rate,

> More than seventy-four percent of home educated adults between the ages of eighteen and twenty-four have taken college-level courses.

and social coping ability. Eight-one percent expect homeschooled students to have about the same GPA as students who attended a traditional high school, and twelve percent expect homeschoolers to have a higher first-year GPA, although many commented that their response was "just a guess" because "we have not looked at this kind of data" or "I do not have direct access to GPAs for comparison." As for retention rates, ninety percent of our survey respondents predict that homeschooled students will have the same or higher retention rate as traditional students; although, again, many commented that they had not specifically looked at this question or did not have access to the relevant data. One admissions officer offered this explanation for higher retention rates among homeschoolers at the college where she works: "The homeschooled applicants we attract tend to be fairly flexible, so when they face obstacles, they either face them head-on or adapt."

The final question in the "expectations" section of our survey asked about how well they expect homeschooled applicants to cope socially in their first year on campus, and the responses strongly suggest that the socialization question discussed in Chapter Three exists in the world of higher education. Only two-thirds of respondents think that homeschoolers will cope as well socially in their first year as traditional students (the lowest percentage in this category for the three performance measures), with almost twenty-eight percent believing they will do worse (by far the highest percentage in the "will do worse" category for all three performance measures). Those that provided comments on this question did not offer any real insight into why they think this, but one admissions officer did explain, "If we have concerns about a student's ability to engage our community the student will likely not be admitted," while another offered, "We have a variety of programs in place to assist students adjust to the university since it's a major transition for all incoming students."

Finally, we asked what recommendations, advice, or general ideas admissions officers think homeschoolers should be aware of. In other words, what would make it easier for admissions officers when considering a homeschooler's application for admission. Our respondents were fairly evenly split on whether or not homeschoolers should plan to attend a community college before entering a four-year college or university, with about a quarter advising "yes" and a third advising "no." However, the largest percentage indicated that they "weren't sure." Sample comments also provided a variety of perspectives on this point, ranging from, "Yes, for dual enrollment purposes," to "Depends on the situation. Homeschool students present a wide array of educational backgrounds. That said, it is helpful if the student has the time and resources to pursue college courses."

Other types of advice provided centered on the major themes of the importance of researching admissions requirements, the value of participating in group activities, and how critical it is to clearly document the course descriptions of the work they have done. The need to provide clear and accurate transcripts, along with grades and course descriptions was actually the most common piece of advice, including comments like, "For my institution, your prior coursework is key. You must meet the same credit requirements and must have a curriculum that would be otherwise accredited." Similarly, another admissions director advised:

> *[H]omeschooled students [should] keep documentation and course descriptions along with grade reporting from the beginning of ninth grade through the end of twelfth grade available for college applications. This grade documentation and course description will help college admissions better assess the student's courses and progress.*

In providing recommendations, some admissions officers also took the opportunity to provide specific words of caution to homeschooled students, while others offered words of encouragement. For example, a member of the admissions team at an elite university shared his personal insight, "It is extremely difficult to be homeschooled and to be properly exposed to advanced levels of STEM in ninth to twelfth grade . . . unless special teaching is involved with lots of resources," while another provided direct advice not to "use a young earth creationist biology curriculum and then apply to a bio or health science related major." Examples of encouraging comments included, "Because homeschooling is less common than schooling in a traditional school setting, it is an opportunity for students to stand out," and:

> *Many colleges and universities will put daunting roadblocks in your way—if you love the schools, try to meet their requirements. But*

know that just because you find obstacles to admission at some schools does not mean you would face those obstacles everywhere. Don't get discouraged.

Conclusion

While many homeschooled students successfully navigate the college admissions process each year, understandably a high level of frustration remains in the homeschooling community as many families still struggle with a lack, or a perceived lack, of clear and consistent criteria, along with limited flexibility in the current admissions process. They are willing to do what is necessary to help their children achieve their higher education goals, but are requesting help in the form of even more detailed information about requirements, additional personal support, and assurances that their children's qualifications will be considered fairly alongside more traditional students' qualifications. Colleges and universities who provide this additional support and clearly welcome qualified homeschooled students are often included on "homeschool-friendly colleges" lists, available on many homeschooling-related websites. The frequency with which these lists are referenced and shared within the homeschooling community indicates the level of concern with which the college admissions process is viewed, and the pervasive impression that numerous schools are "homeschool unfriendly."

On the college side, homeschooled students are generally expected to perform well academically, but concerns remain about social skills and the level of rigor homeschooled students are exposed to with regards to math and science. Also, recommended application materials vary, as do commonly-required documents like transcripts (where the acceptable format can vary) and test scores (which include multiple testing options). Despite this, homeschoolers seem consistently welcome, even encouraged, to apply, at the majority of the schools that participated in our survey.

So, if most homeschooling families want to understand and comply with admissions requirements and recommendations, and most schools are interested in having homeschoolers apply, where is the difficulty? I believe it lies in the wide variety that exists on both sides of the bridge—the variety of homeschooler experiences and the variety of college application requirements for homeschoolers. These variations make it difficult to find common ground that includes clear and consistent requirements across schools, and clear and consistently documented academic achievements. Both sides must continue their attempts to better understand and communicate with the other so that more solid and reliable connections can be made. For admissions officers, this means ensuring a thorough understanding of homeschooling approaches, and awareness of the assumptions and possible misconceptions they may have about these students. For the homeschooling community, this means developing an understanding of the goals and constraints that college counselors and admissions professionals have to balance and navigate. The good news is that these are doable and very much worthwhile, as we will see in the next chapter where we examine how homeschoolers do once they arrive on campus.

Chapter Five

Homeschoolers on Campus . . . and Beyond

Keeping a child out of school deprives him of his essential right to a quality education, including access to tax-funded resources, highly trained teachers and specialists in each discipline, as well as intramural and extracurricular enrichment activities.
~David McGrath, College of DuPage[1]

David McGrath, an English professor at the College of DuPage, continued in his 2016 *Chicago Tribune* commentary:

I felt that the most important benefits missed by stay-at-home kids are socialization from peer group interaction, and the critical thinking and communication skills learned from small- and large-group dynamics in the classroom.

McGrath was like many other professional educators at this point—clearly skeptical of the idea of parents "playing teacher at the kitchen table," and worried about the negative impacts this choice would have on students' learning and development. Then a homeschooled student showed up in the front row of his college-level composition class one day. She had never attended school before college, and yet she was surprisingly successful in Dr. McGrath's course:

> *She maintained eye contact throughout lectures and discussions, listened intently to me and her classmates, raised her hand to offer an observation, an answer, or to ask a question when no one else would, followed instructions to the letter, communicated verbally and in writing more clearly than everyone else and received the highest grade on every assignment.*

His mind was changed. He summarized his impression, concluding, "If every student in my classroom were a radio, my home-schooled student was the one whose switch was turned on." Since that first student, McGrath has taught more than a dozen other home educated students in his classes, and describes them as "competent in social interaction," further observing that "all had already developed their own methods of inquiry for independent learning." He goes on to speculate about the reasons the homeschooled students he has taught are "ideal learners," and proposes the ideas that they "escaped the collateral damage from twelve years of conventional schooling," and that one-on-one learning has allowed them to develop a truly engaged approach, resulting in "plentiful and uninhibited conversation" in his classroom.

Academic Outcomes of Homeschoolers: What the Research Shows

Research backs up McGrath's experiences of homeschoolers performing successfully in the classroom, with multiple studies strongly suggesting that the majority of homeschool graduates who go on to college fare well academically. In 2010, Michael Cogan, Director of Institutional Research and Analysis at the University of St. Thomas, published the results of his research, "Exploring Academic Outcomes of Homeschooled Students," in the *Journal of College Admission*.[2] For this research, he analyzed the academic records of over seventy homeschooled students who entered Wheaton College between 2004 and 2009, and compared them with the records of other students also entering Wheaton in this timeframe, but who had attended public, parochial, or private high schools. He found the homeschooled students:

- Had a higher average ACT score than the overall class (score of 26.5 versus 25.0)

- Had already earned more college credit than the other students prior to entering Wheaton (14.7 credits versus 6.0 credits)

- Had a higher grade point average during their first year of college (3.41 GPA versus 3.12 GPA), and their four-year cumulative GPA was also higher (3.46 GPA versus 3.16 GPA)

- Achieved a higher four-year graduation rate than the overall college population (66.7 percent versus 57.5 percent)

Cogan concluded by saying:

[T]he results provide college admission counselors with further evidence that homeschooled students are prepared for college and may

even be considered as high achievers when compared to non-homeschooled students.

With respect to Cogan's findings on college admissions test scores, and given that ACT and SAT scores are still one of the most-frequently used (if somewhat controversial) measures of college readiness, we should also consider more recent results from the College Board. With over 13,500 homeschooled students taking the SATs in 2014, the College Board reported that homeschoolers earned higher-than-average test scores, with mean scores of 567 in reading and 521 in math, compared to 497 in reading and 513 in math for all college-bound seniors that same year. So, admissions counselors' perceptions that homeschooled students are academically prepared for college (as measured by admissions exams), and will generally do as well or better academically (as measured by college GPAs and graduation rates) compared to traditional students, seem to be accurate. But what about socially? Are admission counselors' concerns that homeschooled students will more likely struggle to adapt socially to their new college environment also correct?

How Homeschoolers Adapt Socially: What the Research Shows

Unlike their academic accomplishments in higher education, less research has been conducted on homeschooler's social transition and integration once they arrive on campus. "Socialization" is a difficult concept to study and measure in a consistent way and, as such, nobody tracks and reports socialization scores that we can compare. An additional challenge is that the population of homeschooled students attending college is still relatively small and widely-dispersed. Further, some studies which have attempted to more fully understand the potential social challenges that homeschoolers face when transitioning to college have significant shortcomings in either the design of their research (with a methodology that included only self-report surveys, for example), or in the sample population studied (like homeschooled students who entered one Catholic university).

One of the few socialization studies to take on this challenge was conducted by Brummond and Wessel in 2012, an often-cited study which specifically explored both the academic and social patterns of homeschooled students through qualitative research.[3] Given the small sample size of their study—six homeschooled students attending the same college—their findings can only be considered as a starting point in understanding homeschoolers' social transitions. They did conclude, however, that these students "experienced college in many of the same ways that other, non-homeschooled students, did."

This conclusion is consistent with another, more recent study that incorporated a larger sample size of homeschoolers. "From Home to Hall," conducted by Dawn Meza Soufleris as her doctoral dissertation at the State University of New York in 2013,[4] twenty-five homeschooled students attending the same university

> *These kids are the epitome of Brown students. They've learned to be self-directed, they take risks, they face challenges with total fervor, and they don't back off.*
>
> ~Joyce Reed, Associate Dean, Brown University

were matched demographically to twenty-five traditional students attending the same university. Through intensive individual interviews with each of the fifty participants, the researcher sought to understand:

- How homeschooled students transitioned to a residential university campus
- How they began to develop the foundations for social capital within the university community
- How their home-based education influenced their ability to cultivate peer relationships, in comparison to conventionally educated students

In the discussion of her results, Soufleris highlighted the gap in perspectives between proponents of homeschooling and its critics that her research sought to address, noting that:

> *Critics of homeschooling have voiced concern that, without formalized elementary and secondary education, students with home-based educational backgrounds will not be sufficiently socially adept to manage the complexities of a university community and student culture.*

With an awareness of these differences, along with her interest in providing a non-biased assessment on the diverging views, the researcher concluded that:

While there were differences between homeschooled and conventionally educated students in my study, the differences were relatively few in terms of their capacities to develop social capital within the university community. Other agents of socialization besides conventional school sites, such as sports groups and youth organizations, religious institutions and homeschool co-ops, and other non-family social outlets provided homeschoolers with the foundations for independent success at university.

Later in her summary, Soufleris also mentioned that the homeschooled students she interviewed were aware of the challenges they would likely face in college before arriving on campus, and "came primed to manage those well, with the goal of countering assumptions they anticipated others would have about their adaptability in college." So, based on the research to date, not only do homeschooled students seem to adapt just as well socially as traditionally-educated students, but they are also aware of the potential difficulties they will face, and arrive on campus prepared to face them (and to prove to others that they are up to the challenge).

Academic and Social Skills Combined: A Look at Academic Self-Efficacy

Self-efficacy for learning is an interesting approach to understanding how well any student, not just homeschooled students, might succeed in the college environment both academically and socially. Academic self-efficacy, or "a person's conviction that they can successfully achieve at a designated level in a specific academic subject area" (as defined by the Institute for Applied Psychometrics) refers to a student's confidence in his academic ability. Confident students are more likely to persist through challenges and be continually motivated by their belief that they can be successful. While multiple factors can affect a person's belief in their ability to thrive academically, including prior academic success and parental feedback, their confidence plays a key role in their ability to relate to teachers and other students in an academic environment. So, a student with low academic self-efficacy is unlikely to believe that he can be successful in a college classroom, whereas conversely, a student with high academic self-efficacy is extremely likely to express confidence in his ability to do well in college (including relating well with professors and peers). So, how do homeschoolers' levels of academic self-efficacy compare to traditional students' levels?

This was one of the central questions investigated by Paul May in 2013 in a study entitled "Listening to the Freshman Voice: First-Year Self-Efficacy and College Expectations Based on High School Types."[5] Specifically, May wanted to know whether first-year college students from four different high school types (public, parochial, private college-prep, and homeschool) differed in their academic self-efficacy. Based on a random sample from the 2009 Beginning College Survey of Student Engagement (BCSSE), which included responses from over 73,000 first-year college students attending almost 200 four-year institutions, he analyzed and compared responses from 681 students who had been homeschooled in high school with responses from approximately 1,000 students from each of the other three high school types. His results were quite clear:

The public's proclivity to lampoon homeschoolers is moot. This study's large sample size, unavailable to previous studies, reveals normality in homeschoolers' perceived academic self-efficacy. The optimism that the future will be bright due to past experiences is unaffected by other factors (communication, gender, etc.). Homeschool graduates perceived the college-going transition with complete competence.

So, based on a study with a large sample size, homeschoolers believe they can do well academically (which requires a high level of social competence to relate effectively with professors and classmates) and, based on studies with smaller sample sizes, these students do manage the transition to college, including the implicit social adjustments and challenges, just as well as other students. If the results of these studies are accurate, we would also expect that retention rates of homeschoolers, which reflect their ability to "fit in" to their college community and be

> One category where homeschoolers tended to outperform their peers from other schooling backgrounds was campus leadership— homeschoolers were significantly more involved in leadership positions for longer periods of time.
>
> ~Kunzman & Gaither, *Homeschooling: A Comprehensive Survey of the Research*

successful year after year until they complete their degree, to be at least as high as the retention rates of traditional students, and we would also expect their college GPAs to be comparable. As we saw in the results of Michael Cogan's research, this is precisely the case. In fact, the four-year graduation rates of homeschoolers in Cogan's study were higher, at 66.7 percent, than the graduation rates of students who had attended public,

Catholic, and private high schools (with four-year graduation rates of 58.6, 54.2, and 51.5 percent, respectively), as were their first-year GPAs and their cumulative four-year GPAs.

Finally, we can also benefit from the observations of those who have directly worked with homeschooled students after they have transitioned to college, including admissions professionals like Gary Mason. In the Fall 2004 edition of the *Journal of College Admission*, in a piece entitled "Homeschool Recruiting: Lessons Learned on the Journey," Mason enthusiastically exclaimed,

> *I love working with homeschoolers! I am a veteran admission professional, and, over the last few years, I have enjoyed working with a new kind of prospective student—those who have been schooled at home during high school. Almost without exception, I have found these students to be friendly, polite, well-prepared, and appreciative of help.*[6]

His experience is not uncommon, as many homeschoolers have had opportunities to interact with people of multiple ages and backgrounds—they have learned how to get along with all kinds of people, an ability that they maintain even after college and into adulthood.

Homeschoolers in Adulthood

In addition to wondering whether students who have been educated at home will be well-educated, socialized, and able to perform successfully in college, some homeschooling skeptics and critics also worry about whether these students will be able to find a job, become active members of their communities, and generally be happy in their adult lives. Much of this book has been dedicated to the first three concerns, but how non-traditional students like homeschoolers function once they reach adulthood is also worth considering. We know that life does not end after college, and it would clearly be in everyone's best interest if homeschooled students grew up to be involved, productive adults after their formal schooling ends—adults who actively participate as engaged citizens and alums, who take on leadership roles in their workplaces and communities. Fortunately, we have some solid research to turn to that gives us a good idea of how homeschoolers turn out.

In 2003, Dr. Brian Ray at the National Home Education Research Institute was asked to research how the first wave of students educated at home in the 1980s and 1990s were managing as adults. He surveyed over 7,000 such adults, including 5,000 who had been homeschooled for seven years or more of their K-12 education. Most of the participants fell between the ages of eighteen and twenty-four, so still quite young, and almost half were full-time students at the time of the survey. Of those who had already begun their careers, the largest number indicated that their work fell into the category of "Professional" (e.g., accountant, registered nurse, artist, doctor, college teacher), with the next most frequent responses including "Homemaker/Home Educator," "Technical" (e.g., computer programmer), or "Office Worker." Other career paths included sales, small business ownership, and trades like mechanics and carpentry.[7] In short, these grown homeschoolers pursued a wide variety of professional occupations.

Ray also asked about other aspects of adulthood related to their general style of living, civic involvement, enjoyment of life, and perspectives on their homeschooling experience. The questions were comparable to questions included on other national surveys, so many of the grown homeschoolers' responses could be compared to national statistics for similar age ranges. When asked about reading habits, and about community involvement in the form of community service and membership in local organizations, nearly one hundred percent of homeschool graduates reported that they had read a book in the past six months (versus two-thirds of similarly-aged adults). Likewise, almost three-quarters had participated in ongoing community service like coaching sports or working with a neighborhood association (versus about a third of the overall group), and nearly twice as many were a member of a church or professional organization compared to their peers. As for civic involvement, less than five percent of homeschool graduates agreed with the statement, "Politics and government are too complicated to understand," while more than a third of the same-age population agreed with that statement. As for voting habits, three-quarters of grown homeschoolers reported that they had voted within the past five years compared to less than a third of their US peers.

In terms of life satisfaction and reflections on their homeschooling experience, it turns out that homeschool graduates are a happy group. Nearly one hundred percent of the respondents reported that they were either "very happy" or "pretty happy," with ninety-five percent glad that they were homeschooled. In fact, a significant majority said that they would homeschool their own children, with three-quarters already doing so. When asked how being homeschooled had affected their lives thus far, nearly all disagreed or strongly disagreed with the statement, "Having been homeschooled has limited my career choices," and agreed or strongly agreed with the statement, "Having been homeschooled is an advantage to me as an adult."

Dr. Peter Gray, a research professor at Boston College, found similarly positive results in his 2013 nationwide study focusing on grown unschoolers (described in Chapter Two).[8] Of the seventy-five qualified respondents who participated in the survey, eighty-three percent had pursued or were pursuing some form of higher education, and almost half had completed a bachelor's degree or higher. Almost all of them reported that they had full-time jobs, and those who were not working were either college students or mothers who were staying at home with their children. Gray notes that a high percentage of this survey group reported careers in creative fields, particularly those who had been unschooled throughout their entire childhood, and an equally high percentage of them were entrepreneurs (with some overlap between these groups). Interestingly, many reported a direct connection between their childhood interests and their field of employment as adults, including one young man who combined his love of nature, photography, and flying into a career as a wilderness aerial photographer. In short, almost all the respondents reported that they were pursuing, or had already found, "enjoyable and meaningful careers."

So how did this group feel about growing up "unschooled"? Overall, the large majority was very happy to have been unschooled, and most reported that they would consider unschooling their own children. Their level of satisfaction with their social lives was high, with most indicating that they had not experienced any difficulties meeting people or making friends. In fact, their level of enthusiasm about unschooling, and the freedom it provided them "to find and pursue their own interests and learn in their own ways" was a consistent theme throughout most of the responses, with some also addressing the additional advantage of unschooling in that it allowed them "to get to know themselves, discover their own passions, and find out how to make their personality work in the world." The primary difficulty they reported had to do with explaining or defending their lifestyle to others who were unfamiliar or skeptical, an issue that almost all homeschoolers regularly confront.

Conclusion

While even the most ardent proponents of homeschooling in all its forms will admit to a wide range in levels of ability within the homeschooling community, as with any group of significant size, most homeschoolers are doing quite well both academically and socially. The transition from home to college to adulthood appears to be seamless for a predominant number of homeschooled students, who largely thrive as they reach adulthood and begin pursuing "enjoyable and meaningful" careers often linked to interests discovered and followed during their homeschooling years. By all accounts, homeschoolers tend to show up on campus as self-directed, self-motivated learners who have a sense of ownership and personal responsibility for their learning and their lives.

Colleges and universities interested in attracting homeschooled applicants to their institutions need to address homeschoolers' unique questions and concerns related to the application process, and to higher education in general. In addition, understanding the wide range of homeschooling approaches, along with some of the misinformation about this alternative form of education, will help college counselors and admissions officers better assess and support these students. Fortunately, some schools have already developed a variety of "homeschool-friendly" processes and policies, and may serve as sources of information and ideas for other institutions interested in connecting more frequently or directly with homeschooled students.

Chapter Six

Attracting and Assessing Homeschooled Students: A Survey of Common and Best Practices

During my years working as a management consultant, one of the common strategies for helping companies improve their processes and implement new systems was to conduct "best practices" research, using those findings to develop recommendations for our clients on how they might solve a particular problem or reach a selected goal. Whether they wanted to restructure their compensation system, update to a new human resources management system, or entirely reorganize their company, we usually began the project by looking within the client's industry to understand and compare how other companies had approached a similar issue, and we also often looked outside the industry at comparable companies in different lines of business. We did not want to reinvent the wheel every time a new process or system was implemented—we wanted to save time and money and quickly achieve more effective results by learning from others' successes and mistakes. This is not to say that what worked for one organization would work for another, as modifications and some level of customization were usually required based on factors such as differences in size, culture, and overall organizational goals.

However, taking the time to research and compare different approaches despite these differences resulted in a high return on the investment in time and resources.

So, during the late summer and early fall of 2016, I decided to conduct some best practices research focusing on college admissions for homeschoolers with the goal of developing a set of insights and recommendations that would benefit colleges and university admissions offices interested in increasing the number of homeschoolers they attract and enroll. This research primarily consisted of interviews with a variety of admissions officers working within different colleges and universities that regularly recruit and enroll non-traditional students like homeschoolers and have, based on their websites, interesting or uncommon application requirements and guidelines for homeschoolers. I attempted to include a variety of schools—some of them test-optional, some not; some small or private, some larger or public—but each with an intentional and specific strategy for working with homeschoolers before and during the admissions process.

I asked admissions professionals, usually a director or assistant director of admissions, to describe their process for evaluating homeschooled applicants' files, including detailing which documents were required or simply recommended. I also asked them to indicate which part of the process was different for homeschooled students than for traditional students, and then concluded each interview by asking them to pose a question that would provide information to make their jobs easier or to help them do their jobs better. After compiling a list of these questions, and depending on the type of information being sought, I either sent out a request to the greater homeschooling community for their input (usually through the larger online communities), or included these questions in subsequent interviews with members of the admissions community. In no particular order, the most frequently-asked questions posed by admissions professionals were:

- Do other schools have separate review processes for homeschoolers and, if so, what does that look like, especially in terms of measurables?

- How do homeschoolers do once on campus?

- How do institutions maintain compliance with federal regulations regarding financial aid as it relates to homeschool students?

- In assessing curriculum that is non-standard, how are other schools doing this? Are they prompting applicants in a way that leads to clearer information? Are there tools?

- Are there unique ways that others work with homeschool students? (As one admissions director said, "We always want to be innovating.")

- Where do I find more homeschoolers?

Based on the information I gathered throughout these interviews, in addition to some additional secondary research, here are some answers about common and best practices that may prove useful, or at least interesting, to everyone involved in college admissions.

Do other schools have separate review processes for homeschoolers and, if so, what does that look like, especially in terms of measurables?

I did not come across any schools with a completely separate process for homeschoolers, although almost every admissions officer I spoke with described a process that they have adapted in some way. Most commonly, the adaptation consists of a different "lens" through which homeschoolers' transcripts are evaluated and often involves designating one staff member as the primary contact person and reader for homeschooler files (although others on the committee do read them). Also, to make up for other traditional information that may be lacking, an extra step, such as additional testing or writing samples, is often required of homeschooled applicants.

One example of a school that incorporates each of these adaptations in their process is a well-respected, private liberal arts college in the Midwest that received applications from almost forty homeschoolers in 2015. This school just recently reorganized their admissions staff so that they no longer recruit students and review files based on

> By the time they arrive in our classes, many Berkeley undergraduates are absolute Matajuros [sword masters] of test-taking. It's no wonder we're gravely disappointed—and they're resentfully surprised—when we ask them to actually be apprentice scientists or scholars instead. Skilled adults continue to face difficult challenges, of course, but passing exams isn't one of them. Being the best test-taker in the world isn't much help for discovering either new truths about that world or new ways of thriving in it.
>
> ~Alison Gopnik, The Gardener and the Carpenter

assigned geographic territories, but rather on special populations, one of which is homeschoolers. As an admissions officer from this school explained, "We realize that a student from California is not just a student from California; they are also an athlete or an aspiring biology major, so we've reorganized around this idea to try to be more effective." Once she begins reading homeschoolers' files, she looks for "strong evidence of inquiry" and for "evidence that they will be able to thrive in a traditional academic setting," unique lenses that do not carry the same level of importance for traditional applicants. And although this school does not require standardized test scores for traditional students, they do require them for homeschooled students if they have not graduated from an accredited, diploma-granting organization (an example of an additional step homeschoolers must take).

Another example of other lenses and requirements includes an admissions officer from a private university in the southeast who shared that when reading files from homeschoolers, he looks for evidence of how they have taken advantage of the freedom and flexibility provided by homeschooling to explore interesting and unique opportunities and to challenge themselves. In terms of additional steps or requirements, these vary widely as many schools require, or strongly recommend, items like extra essays or letters of recommendation, reading lists, SAT subject tests, interviews, or writing samples. So, while these schools do not have entirely separate review processes for homeschoolers, they do have modified review processes.

How do homeschoolers do once on campus?

Few (if any) colleges or universities have the time or resources to track how well homeschooled students do throughout their four years on their campus, but it is natural for those who have so closely considered these students' applications and likelihood for college success to wonder how they actually fare. The best information available to answer this question is provided by the studies described and summarized in Chapter Five, which consistently indicate that college students who were homeschooled do just as well, if not better, on multiple measures of success throughout college: grades, social adaptation, and graduation rates. However, it may be worthwhile to take this opportunity to consider the question from another angle and ask, "Why do homeschooled students tend to do well in college?"

Researchers who have focused on this question frequently show correlation, not causation, so we can only make some reasonable guesses about the possible answers at this point. Many have speculated that homeschooled students who attend college do well because they are more likely to have well-educated parents, and to come from families with more financial resources. Others have speculated that these students are successful in higher education because their earlier education was tailored to their abilities and interests, often supported by one-on-one or small group instruction. If we look closely at each of these possibilities, we can see that each of these factors has one thing in common: engagement.

Parents who decide to leave a well-established educational system to educate their children at home clearly do so because they want to provide a higher-quality learning environment and education for their children. This is supported by the NCES research cited earlier which indicates that "concern about the school environment" and "dissatisfaction with academic instruction" are two of the leading reasons many families decide to homeschool. In other words, homeschooling parents are engaged in their children's education and, as a result, their children receive a clear message about the value of education. This message influences the students, too, leading to a higher level of engagement for them. Consequently, many homeschool students, especially once they reach their teen years, end up directing their own education and spending more time exploring and learning about topics and skills that interest them, and pursuing learning methods that suit their particular learning preferences. Since most home educated students can academically keep up with their school-aged peers by doing three or four hours of school work per day, they have plenty of time to customize their education and pursue their individual passions, with engagement in what they are learning a natural result. We see evidence of this in the terms that are frequently used to describe homeschooled students, including "self-directed students," "independent learners," and "motivated students."

Gallup confirms the importance of engagement in achieving positive learning outcomes, listing it as one of the key factors in academic success. In fact, engagement is one of the concepts measured in Gallup's Student Poll, a twenty-question survey of over 800,000 students attending public schools in grades five through twelve, that measures several academic success factors "that drive students' grades, achievement scores, retention, and future employment." Gallup defines engagement this way: "The involvement in and enthusiasm for school which reflects how well students are known and how often they get to do what they do best."

Feeling "known" and getting to do "what they do best" are two of the most frequently listed benefits of homeschooling, which also serve as a point of differentiation between homeschoolers' educational experiences and those of many of their peers attending public schools. According to Gallup's 2014 Student Poll (mentioned in Chapter One), almost half of students enrolled in public schools are either "not engaged" (twenty-eight percent) or are "actively disengaged" (nineteen percent) in school. If we focus on just high school juniors and seniors—those who are applying to college or preparing to enter college—the average level of engagement is even lower. Specifically, public school students in the last two years of high school had the fewest number of students reporting that they "have the opportunity to do what they do best every day," or indicating that they "have received recognition or praise for doing good schoolwork," or even believing that their school "is committed to building the strengths of each student."[1]

So, engagement is clearly something we need to foster in all students if we want to provide them with the best chances for academic success. And it appears that homeschooled students may have an advantage in this area over the average traditionally-schooled student, which may, at least partially, explain why homeschoolers tend to do well in college: They have had more freedom to identify and pursue their interests, to cultivate a love of learning, and to develop their personal and academic strengths in the process.

How do institutions maintain compliance with federal regulations regarding financial aid as it relates to homeschool students?

This is a very important question for both homeschoolers and admissions officers alike, and both sides have experienced confusion regarding exactly what is required to qualify for federal financial aid.

According to Federal Student Aid, an office of the US Department of Education, students applying for federal aid must show that they are qualified "to obtain a college or career school education" through one of the following options:

- Having a high school diploma or a recognized equivalent such as a General Educational Development (GED) certificate
- Completing a high school education in a *homeschool* setting approved under state law (or—if state law does not require a homeschooled student to obtain a completion credential—completing a high school education in a homeschool setting that qualifies as an exemption from compulsory attendance requirements under state law)
- Enrolling in an eligible career pathway program and meeting one of the "ability-to-benefit" alternatives[2]

The second option, "completing a high school education in a home school setting approved under state law," seems to present the most confusion, probably because this was the most recently added provision through the Higher Education Amendments of 1998. It did not help that this amendment was incorrectly interpreted and described in the Federal Student Aid Handbook in 2001, so many admissions officers and financial aid officers were misinformed about the actual federal requirements, and remain confused. Specifically, some college administrators and admissions representatives have interpreted this second option to mean that homeschoolers who do not have either an accredited transcript from a public or private school, or a GED, must provide evidence (usually a letter) from their educational school district confirming that the student is exempt from compulsory attendance. *This is not the case.* According to one of the authors of the 1998 amendment:

> Any students, of any age, who have graduated from any high school—whether public, non-public, or homeschool—are outside the compulsory attendance requirements imposed by their state statutes. Homeschool graduates need only to demonstrate that they have successfully completed a secondary school education in a home school setting and have met state law requirements.
>
> ~Home School Legal Defense Association

On the issue of proof of their completion of a homeschool program, the Handbook says on page 6 of Volume 2, chapter 1 that an institution "may rely on a home-schooled student's self-certification that he or she completed secondary school in a home school setting."[3]

As for the definition of "compulsory attendance":

The Department considers a homeschooled student to be beyond the age of compulsory attendance if your school's state would not require the student to further attend secondary school or continue to be homeschooled.[4]

So, homeschoolers can self-certify through a parent-created transcript that they have completed their secondary education in compliance with their particular state's regulations, and are considered to be exempt from compulsory attendance once they have completed their

> *Some colleges and universities have incorrectly interpreted the Higher Education Act amendment language to mean that each college carries the burden of proof to determine the legality of a particular home school applicant's "home school setting." Contrary to this understanding, educational institutions carry no such burden.*
>
> ~Home School Legal Defense Association

homeschool secondary education, regardless of their age. No further proof is required to receive federal financial aid for the student, and the school's institutional eligibility for federal funds is not endangered.

In short, the news is good for everyone: a parent-created high school transcript is frequently (depending on the state) all that is necessary.

In assessing curriculum that is non-standard, how are other schools doing this?

Many colleges and universities face the challenge of designing and implementing a fair and efficient process for evaluating non-traditional, non-standardized applications, especially as the number of homeschooled applicants continues to grow. Test-optional schools find this even more difficult, as they have eliminated one of the standard measures of comparison. What's more, whichever approach schools adopt, the assessment system needs to be one that can easily be described to potential homeschooled applicants so they understand the school's requirements and what educational choices they need to consider in order to submit a competitive application.

One university shared with an independent college advisor (who is also a homeschooling parent) how they assesses their applicants and the difficulty this admissions officer has in applying their school's standard process to non-traditional applications, especially those who may not have taken courses outside of their homeschool program:

My university is looking to create a set of guidelines to help counselors better review home schooled students. Currently, all students are recalculated and put on an unweighted 4.0 scale. Their rigor is evaluated through a process we call strength of curriculum. It is on a scale of 1-10. The number 6 is given to students who have taken a college preparatory level throughout high school. The number goes up based on number of honors/AP courses taken versus what is available. An example of this is a student on the IB scale might get a 10 because we understand the rigor of the academics. However, with the varying types of homeschool programs (some are unregulated), it is hard to effectively evaluate this constituent group. The students who fare the best are those who have taken course work outside of the homeschool program such as at a community college. We are a test-optional institution but SAT/ACT scores help this student in our committee review. Do you have recommendations for us?

So, for students who have few, if any, standard measures of academic ability like certified transcripts and grade point averages, college entrance exam scores, or other class grades or test scores, knowing how to assess their level of readiness for college and how likely they are to succeed is difficult. What a variety of schools have found in this situation is that the school profile/counselor letter provided by the family is the key to gaining the necessary insight into the family's educational philosophy and approach as they include specific information on their reason(s) for homeschooling, the parents' perspectives on education, and the number of years the student has been homeschooled. For students from families who clearly value and prioritize education,

> Among the nation's elite universities, Stanford has been one of the most eager to embrace [homeschooled students]. Despite the uncertainties of admitting students with no transcripts or teacher recommendations, the University welcomes at least a handful every year. Stanford has found that the brightest homeschoolers bring a mix of unusual experiences, special motivation and intellectual independence that makes them a good bet to flourish on the Farm.
>
> ~"Stanford Alumni Magazine," Nov/Dec 2000

the information provided related to these three factors can be assumed to reflect the quality of the education their child has attained. For example, a student who has been homeschooled in order to take advantage of deeper or broader learning opportunities in unique environments, and whose parents are college-educated or have demonstrably dedicated themselves to providing and facilitating enriching educational options, is highly likely to be an engaged, resilient, and self-directed college student.

In addition to the homeschool profile and parent letter, homeschool transcripts, even those created by the families themselves, can be of significant value in the assessment process. Admittedly, grades assigned by the parents can be suspect if they provide only one person's perspective of the student's academic abilities. Grade inflation exists everywhere, though, even in public and private high schools, so looking more closely at the course sequences and descriptions, along with related work samples and reading lists, can help in assessing the rigor and depth of a student's educational process. Self-directed interests that have been pursued over a sustained period, with resultant work products or letters from tutors, mentors, or other advisors, can often be assumed to have had the same level of rigor as honors or advanced placement courses.

Some schools, including a public liberal arts college in the Pacific Northwest, have decided to take homeschool transcripts "at face value" and, while they do require submission of ACT or SAT test scores, they do not set a minimum score for admission. In addition to looking closely at the school profile/counselor letter and transcript, the director of admissions says, "We tend to lean more heavily on a homeschooled student's essays and writing ability when reviewing their application, as well as their resume, which can reflect their community involvement." He goes on to explain that his admissions team looks for a "hook," something that makes the student interesting and shows how they have maximized the opportunities provided by the additional freedom and flexibility of their homeschooling lifestyle.

Another liberal arts school in the Pacific Northwest has recently introduced a portfolio option for admissions, in addition to their standard process, that attracts many non-traditional students since it does not require students to submit test scores (although students can provide those if they choose). Students who decide to apply via the portfolio path still need to submit a transcript with grades and letters of recommendation, and then must submit one graded analytic work (usually an English or social studies paper) and one graded science or quantitative work sample. The combination of the transcript, letters of recommendation, and work samples provides the admissions team with something objective to consider (the graded work samples) along with insights into the student's "chronology of approach," allowing the school to consider the student "in the context of their educational environment."

So, while non-standard curriculum can present challenges for those who work in admissions, there are methods for credibly assessing a student's educational accomplishments and academic abilities. Most admissions officers confirm that it helps if the student has taken at least a few graded outside courses and can provide test scores, whether AP, CLEP, or ACT/SAT scores. Increasingly, however, admissions officers are discovering that non-quantitative methods for assessing a student's qualifications can be just as effective. Regardless of the approach adopted, however, keep in mind the conclusions of some of the research described in the prior chapters and note a couple of important points:

1. No correlation exists between homeschool regulations or parent certification as a teacher and the academic achievements of a homeschooled student.
2. Students from unregulated, unaccredited homeschools perform equally well in college as traditional students do—across all measures of success.

Are there unique ways that others work with homeschool students?

As I have been speaking with and getting to know a growing number of admissions officers, the one thing most of them have in common is a strong interest in learning about what others in their community are doing. As one assistant director of admissions told me, "I always want to be innovating," and another shared, "I'd really love to know how other schools are assessing curriculum that is non-standard. Are they prompting [students] in some way to provide information differently? Are there tools that can help?"

Since we addressed the issue of assessing non-standard curriculum in the prior question, let us now focus on the ideas of innovation and other unique approaches to working with non-traditional students like homeschoolers. A few examples of interesting approaches that stood out in my conversations with admissions officers follow.

Portfolio Options

A sizeable number of schools offer portfolio options, and more are beginning to offer this path as an alternative to the standard admissions process in an effort to increase college access for a wider variety of students, allowing students who have participated in project-based learning to show what they have accomplished beyond just grades and test scores. MIT is a notable example of a school that implemented a portfolio-based "Maker Portfolio" undergraduate admissions option. After two years of providing this option, they reported:

> *In many respects, the Maker Portfolio has been a resounding success. Over the last two years, more than 2,000 students have used it to show us the things they make, from surfboards to solar cells, code to cosplay, prosthetics to particle accelerators. We believe the Maker Portfolio has improved our assessment of these applicants*

and offers us a competitive advantage over our peers who have not developed the processes to identify and evaluate this kind of talent.

Online Transcript Creator

One of the big challenges that homeschoolers face when applying to college is creating a transcript which thoroughly and succinctly reflects their educational accomplishments and also meets the varying formatting requirements of the schools they are applying to. Some schools accept, and even expect, narrative transcripts from homeschoolers, while others require a more standard transcript supported by some combination of supplementary documents, which may include detailed course descriptions, book lists, writing samples, or other work products. A few schools, including the University of South Florida, have recognized how challenging this aspect of the admissions process can be for homeschoolers and have begun including an online transcript template on their website for home educated applicants. This template removes any doubt that homeschoolers might have about whether they are providing the appropriate type and level of information. Homeschoolers who have used this tool express appreciation and give it rave reviews.

Unique Essay Prompts

For schools looking for creative, out-of-the-box thinkers (as many homeschoolers pride themselves on being), providing unusual and thought-provoking essay prompts allows them to get to know their applicants in ways that standard essays and quantitative metrics might not. The University of Chicago is one example of a school providing uncommon and "fun" supplemental essay prompts as part of its standard admissions process. Unusual questions like these appeal to non-traditional students who often spend lots of time developing their creative abilities and exploring the world driven by their highly individual and unique interests, and are eager to share their uncommon insights and perspectives. Here are some examples from their admissions page:

- What is square one, and can you actually go back to it?

- The ball is in your court—a penny for your thoughts, but say it, don't spray it. So long as you don't bite off more than you can chew, beat around the bush, or cut corners, writing this essay should be a piece of cake. Create your own idiom, and tell us its origin—you know, the whole nine yards. PS: A picture is worth a thousand words.

- Alice falls down the rabbit hole. Milo drives through the tollbooth. Dorothy is swept up in the tornado. Neo takes the red pill. Don't tell us about another world you've imagined, heard about, or created. Rather, tell us about its portal. Sure, some people think of the University of Chicago as a portal to their future, but please choose another portal to write about.

Non-Traditional Admissions at Non-Traditional Schools

We have just seen three examples of unique approaches some schools are taking to attract and assess homeschooled applicants, but to answer this question even more fully, I thought it might be valuable to explore the admissions processes of other non-traditional schools and programs which also recruit recently-graduated high school students, including those who have been homeschooled. For this, I researched two program, the first offered by Praxis, an intense apprentice-based program that combines formal instruction, individual coaching, and experiential learning into a nine-month experience resulting in a job for the apprentices at the end of the program. The second is Minerva, which offers "an innovative undergraduate program that combines four years of world travel with rigorous, interdisciplinary study." Both Praxis and Minerva describe their admissions processes as highly selective, and report that they are seeking candidates with a strong combination of intellectual ability, critical thinking skills, and personal attributes that support working effectively within teams—common skills and abilities that most colleges and universities also seek in their applicants.

The apprenticeship program offered by Praxis recruits a variety of applicant types, ranging from highly-motivated recent high school graduates who are interested in gaining practical skills and work experience, to young entrepreneurs seeking experience and connections before launching their own business, to college graduates with several years of work experience who want to take their career in a new direction. The competitive admissions process is comprised of multiple stages throughout which applicants are assessed based on four key factors: character, intelligence, experience, and skills. The first stage involves completing an application, submitting a resume, and providing written responses to questions about the applicant's talents, skills, and goals. Those who appear to be a good fit for the program are invited to proceed to the second phase, where they are asked to submit a real-world writing sample (examples include a blog post, a professional email, or a published article), letters from two professional references, and recorded video responses to two questions which candidates select from a list. Applicants who proceed to the third and final phase are asked to participate in two live, one-on-one interviews with different Praxis team members who make final determinations on whether each candidate is a good fit for the program. Those who are ultimately accepted into the program have demonstrated through the three phases of application that they bring a solid mix of skills, experiences, and attitudes that will add a valuable apprentice for their business partners.

The admissions process at Minerva is also a merit-based, multi-step process "designed to discover who you are and what you are passionate about." As a new school, the founding team had the opportunity to develop their admissions process from scratch, and pulled heavily from available research during their design process. What they determined was that college entrance test scores are not good predictors student success, so Minerva does not accept SAT/ACT test scores. They do, however, ask applicants to provide the details of their academic history, accept the Common Application, and focus on getting to know applicants on personal level during this first "Who You Are" phase of the admissions process through supplemental essays and information. The second phase focuses on gaining an understanding of how the applicant thinks, and is comprised of a series of online timed "thought-provoking" challenges designed to measure applicants' creativity, critical thinking skills, math knowledge, and written and verbal communication abilities. The admissions director summarized, "We need to know what level of rigor this student is capable of." The third and final phase allows applicants to demonstrate what they have achieved, both academically and otherwise. Their high school grades are one point of consideration, and other non-academic accomplishments are equally considered and can include a wide variety of experiences and projects.

What both Minerva and Praxis have in common is that both of their processes are holistic and primarily qualitatively focused. Each organization has designed a process to objectively assess applicants without relying on test scores, grades, and standardized curriculums, instead focusing on current capabilities, talents, and personal attributes as demonstrated through critical thinking challenges, work products, and interviews. While their admissions processes are more time-intensive than those at traditional colleges and universities, both admissions directors I spoke with emphasized that the extra investment of time has helped them get to know their applicants and effectively select highly qualified candidates who have gone on to be very successful in their respective programs.

Where do I find more homeschoolers?

I love this question, as do other homeschoolers. We all want to be sought after, right? After hearing this question, or some version of it, from a variety of admissions officers, I decided to ask a community of homeschoolers who have high-school-aged kids where and how they prefer to be "found," and the responses were quite varied (as you might expect from a group of homeschoolers). Some families who attend homeschooling conferences said they would like to find information about colleges at these events,

> The first step is for colleges to have the needed information readily available on their websites. I am immediately turned away if I can't find information about CLEP exams, transfer credits, etc.
>
> ~Homeschooling Parent

while many others said they never attend conferences and would prefer to be found online, maybe through state homeschool association sites or Facebook groups. Campus tours dedicated to homeschoolers, or homeschool Q&A events (online or in person) were also suggested as options that people would be interested in. Overwhelmingly, one request emerged again and again: through a page just for homeschoolers on the college's website.

Homeschooling parents are generally very comfortable doing research—they have been doing it for years as they research state homeschooling regulations, curriculum options, sources for art or lab materials, book lists, local classes and co-ops, and internship and volunteer opportunities. In fact, homeschooling parents have extensive experience with researching and finding information. Unsurprisingly, when it becomes clear that college is in their child's future, researching schools and admissions requirements is just the "next thing on the list."

This is where some real frustration sets in for many parents and students, as they hunt around multiple college websites in search of information on required courses, tests, and documents. Often, when they do locate the relevant section or page for homeschoolers, they find that many of the questions they are seeking answers to are not addressed. Questions like, "How do you treat CLEP credits earned by homeschoolers?" and "If my student took community college classes for high school, will those credits be accepted?" are some of the more common concerns. In addition, many families want to know what the institution's preferred transcript format is, and whether there are other documents that the admissions staff recommends for their students to best demonstrate their qualifications. Many homeschooling parents and students are also trying to gauge how "homeschool-friendly" a college or university might be as they wonder whether they will be welcome in their classes and "fit in" on campus.

Thoroughness of information, contact information for an admissions representative, and the general tone of the site can help convey how interested an institution is in receiving applications from homeschoolers and can encourage homeschoolers to consider applying to the school. When I surveyed a national group of homeschooling parents about which schools do a particularly good job of describing the application process and their requirements for homeschoolers, they pointed to the websites of these seven schools:

American University

Homeschoolers are clearly welcome at this university, as reflected in the friendly tone and clear descriptions of what is required and what is optional to apply, and the contact link for those with further questions.

Brandeis University

The page for homeschoolers provides a succinct, clear list of required documents, plus a link that takes the applicant to a page where they can sign up for an interview with a Brandeis representative.

Cedarville University

The homeschooler page includes quotes from homeschooled students who attended the school, reasons why homeschoolers should consider the school, and answers to homeschoolers' frequently asked questions.

Denison University

This university's page for homeschooled applicants is brief, but provides clear academic requirements, document requirements, and interview requirements.

Radford University

This school breaks out their requirements for homeschoolers into categories, depending on the homeschoolers' program, along with several options for demonstrating academic proficiency in math and English.

University of South Florida

In addition to providing a clear description of the special requirements for homeschoolers, this site also includes an additional page detailing the additional factors they consider during the admissions process for homeschoolers, along with an online transcript creator tool.

University of Washington

This school's site includes multiple pages of information for homeschoolers and a main page providing an overview of admissions requirements with links to information on transfer credits, dual enrollment programs, and a description of their holistic review process.

Conclusion

Over the course of the last three chapters we have taken a closer look at the concerns homeschoolers have and the challenges they face as they apply to college, examined how well they do once they arrive on campus, and surveyed some of the common practices that colleges and universities across the country have implemented to better serve these non-traditional students. While most of these common or unique admissions practices cost very little to implement or maintain—from modifying admissions requirements and processes, to updating the admissions website—they can have a big impact on how homeschool-friendly a college or university is perceived to be. Because homeschoolers often lack the assistance of professional guidance counselors to help them through the search and application process, if a school's requirements place extra hurdles in the application path for homeschoolers, whether these are additional tests or insufficient detail on the website, these students are more likely to feel that the school may not be interested in accepting them and will decide not to apply.

Based on my research with admissions officers, however, it appears that the vast majority of schools do welcome homeschoolers and want them to apply. Based on the experiences and frustrations expressed by homeschoolers who have been or are going through the process, though, many colleges and universities still have room to improve their outreach and messages to homeschoolers if they are truly interested in tapping into this growing population of potential applicants. We have already touched on some of the steps admissions officers can take, and we have a few more to add for those who are interested in expanding their attraction and recruitment efforts, and making their processes even more efficient.

Chapter Seven

Taking Action: Recommendations for Recruiting and Assessing Homeschoolers

For the first time in more than a decade, the United States faces an overall decrease in the number of American high-school graduates. Developing strategies for attracting and recruiting a largely untapped market of qualified and highly-motivated students like homeschoolers could help many schools close the gap in their enrollment targets. Admissions officers interested in connecting and communicating with these non-traditional students need to incorporate non-traditional approaches in the recruiting and admissions processes based on an updated understanding of the homeschooling movement and the challenges that homeschooling families face. Most homeschoolers willingly and happily comply with whatever requirements colleges have in place; they just need to know specifically what admissions officers want, and have a general sense that the process is fair, which signals that they will be welcome on campus.

In the previous chapter we touched on some of the steps that several institutions of higher education have taken, including some non-traditional programs, to facilitate the research and application process for homeschoolers. In this final chapter we will summarize these options and add a few more worth considering.

Recruiting Options

Expanding the Admissions Website

For students who are largely working on their own during the college research and application process, or who have unique interests and concerns, a welcoming and detailed admissions website is perhaps the best way to make a positive first impression. Providing clear answers to non-traditional questions, such as how community college credits earned during high school are handled, recommended CLEP and SAT subject tests and how they will be considered, transcript templates or tools, suggestions for how to include homeschool-specific information on the Common Application, and financial aid and scholarship information will be much appreciated. Homeschoolers also appreciate insights from other homeschoolers enrolled at the school, program-specific information highlighting items that may be of interest to homeschoolers (like project-based classes, or the opportunity to design their own major), and contact information for a designated homeschool specialist on the admissions team.

Attending Homeschooling Conferences

Numerous homeschooling conferences and conventions are held every year throughout the country, and many homeschooling families attend these events regularly. (See Appendix B for a list of some of the larger and better-known conferences.) Some are organized by state homeschooling organizations, others are presented by regional or national homeschooling support groups, and all present a wide variety of workshops and resources for homeschooling families of all types. College admissions representatives are almost always welcome, and are often invited to provide a presentation or serve on a panel, making these events a great way to connect with both parents and students.

Connecting with Homeschooling Organizations

Writing articles, placing ads, or announcing events through some of the larger homeschooling organizations and websites can be another great way to connect with the homeschooling community. Numerous homeschool support organizations maintain active Facebook pages, websites, digital magazines, newsletters, and blogs. A list of just a few of the larger of these organizations can be found in Appendix B.

Educating the Admissions Staff

Many homeschooling parents have expressed frustration about calling the admissions office and not being able to find anyone who could answer their questions, or meeting a school representative at a college fair who was not aware of the application requirements or process for homeschoolers, or who provided different answers than another admissions representative from the same school. Ensuring that everyone in the admissions office who might be contacted by an interested homeschooler knows your school's policies and can answer questions accurately will help increase the probability that interested homeschool students will apply to your school.

Creating Events for Homeschoolers and Other Non-Traditional Students

Homeschoolers seek events designed specifically for homeschoolers, like campus visits or webinars, especially if they include current students attending the university who were previously homeschooled. Schools that offer personalized events like these can help homeschoolers and other non-traditional students feel that they will be welcome on campus and will fit in with the campus community.

Including Homeschoolers in Outreach to Transfer Students

Homeschooled students frequently take advantage of dual enrollment or early college programs which allow them to take classes at local college community colleges while they are still in high school. By the time they finish high school, many of these students have accumulated enough college credits to qualify as transfer students to many colleges and universities. If your school already has an outreach plan for transfer students, consider adding home educated students to this plan, including connecting with them during your campus visits and creating information specifically for them in your marketing materials.

Connecting with Other Homeschoolers on Campus

Allowing potential homeschool applicants to connect with other homeschoolers who have already enrolled at your school, whether at in-person events or online, helps homeschoolers get a better idea of how well they might fit in at your school. Many homeschoolers wonder what it will be like to attend college-level classes, and whether other students will think they are "weird" because they did not attend a traditional high school. Speaking with homeschooled students who have already made the transition can help alleviate these concerns.

Application Options

Offering a Modified Process for Homeschoolers

Offering a modified process for homeschooled applicants can either include an "add on" option, or an entirely separate path to admissions. The first would require applicants to submit all regularly-required documents, but would also provide them with the option to include additional items like portfolios of completed work, lists of books read, or interviews with admissions staff. The second might look similar to the one offered by the private school described in the previous chapter, which replaces test scores with a portfolio path of graded work products. For each of these you might also consider allowing homeschooled applicants to provide an expanded list and descriptions of extracurricular activities since it is often difficult for them to draw a line between "extracurricular" and "school"—internships, volunteering, and part-time jobs are frequently incorporated as applied learning in many homeschooling curriculums. Likewise, providing an opportunity to submit a recorded presentation on a topic or project the student is excited about will afford you the chance to get to know this applicant better, to see their accomplishment and learn about their passions.

Removing Hurdles

Homeschoolers tend to shy away from colleges that put up extra hurdles for them, perceiving these hurdles as an indirect message that their educational accomplishments may not be considered valid, and therefore they may not be welcome on campus. Review your current process and the additional requirements placed on homeschoolers with an eye toward how much value the extra steps provide in helping you assess homeschooled applicants' qualifications. If you find these additional requirements valuable and necessary, consider providing an explanation on the homeschooling section of your website of how they are used in the admissions process. If you can, eliminate or modify steps that do not add much value. This may make the process more efficient for everyone, allowing applicants to focus on the aspects of the process that provide you the most helpful information.

Designating a Homeschool Specialist

Some schools have found it worthwhile and easy to select a person on the admissions team who serves as the primary point of contact for homeschoolers and other non-traditional applicants. Designating someone familiar with (or who can research) different state requirements, and who can spend some additional time reviewing these unique, and often more complex, applications makes the application process smoother and more effective for everyone. Also, many homeschoolers say that they appreciate having someone they can contact directly with their questions and that these interactions help them get a better feel for the school and how well they might fit in there.

Providing a Transcript Template

Very few traditional students ever think about transcript formats, but for homeschoolers this part of the college application process represents significant concern, particularly for those who have pursued a less-structured approach to education. Compressing what and how they have learned over four years into a standard format with clearly-delineated courses is difficult, and often leaves out significant activities and accomplishments. Providing an example of your preferred transcript format, or of format options, alleviates some of this concern, and can help ensure that you receive the information you need in a more consistent manner across applicants. Also, if you do not already, consider allowing non-traditional students to provide narrative transcripts, which allow these students to more thoroughly describe their learning experiences and accomplishments.

Taking a Holistic View of Homeschooled Applicants

Prioritizing grades, course sequences, and test scores may not allow your team to gain a thorough perspective of non-traditional students, as these elements of education tend not to be a priority for many homeschoolers. Even if you cannot modify your requirements or process, adopting a more holistic perspective of a non-traditional student's experiences and qualifications may help your admissions team appreciate the diverse set of knowledge and skills that a homeschooled student can bring to your school. Evaluating homeschooling statements, letters of recommendation, work portfolios, reading lists, interviews, and essays equally with other parts of the application may give you a better sense of the student's true abilities and potential.

Adding Unique Essay Prompts

Homeschoolers tend to be highly creative and, because of their entrepreneurial approach to education, also tend to have uncommon perspectives and ideas. Allowing them to demonstrate their creativity and unique insights through unusual essay prompts will help you gain a clearer picture of how a homeschooled applicant might positively contribute in their classes and to their peers.

Assessment Options

Considering Potential Biases

When I asked one admissions officer what her recommendation would be to others in admissions regarding homeschooled students, she said, "Invest in making the evaluation process as objective as possible. We should work from the assumption that talent exists everywhere, it's not concentrated in any one applicant type." She further emphasized, "It's important to give applicants who do not fit the traditional mold a chance to shine." Other admissions officers mentioned similar ideas.

One admissions officer who had worked at several schools, beginning with a very homeschool-friendly school and then moving to another school less open to non-traditional students, shared that a key question for him when reviewing applications from homeschoolers is, "Where is the burden of proof going to be on any given part of the application?" He decided that it needs to be on the admissions counselor, whose job it is to work with the homeschooler to gather and understand everything necessary to fully evaluate their qualifications:

> *In higher education the assumption is that homeschool students are not qualified and that we need to require extra details and proof. What we really need to do is shift our perspective and train our counselors to challenge their own potential biases.*

134

Understandably, many higher education faculty and administrators have some level of bias about homeschoolers. After all, most Americans have twelve to sixteen years of traditional school experience, making it difficult to imagine that any other approach to education might result in equally-qualified students. It may help to remember that homeschooling is legal in all fifty states, that homeschoolers tend to do quite well academically, and that "unregulated" does not mean "out of compliance." Homeschoolers highly value education, and appreciate the freedom to choose the best educational method for their children, so they tend to go to great lengths to make sure they are always in compliance with their state's regulations.

Looking for Other Success Factors

Like the admissions officer whose information request I shared in the prior chapter, many admissions officers struggle with the challenge of reviewing files from homeschooled students who have pursued a non-standard curriculum. Again, taking a more holistic approach and weighing other elements of the application more heavily for these students is one approach to this issue, and it may also be helpful to look for evidence of other success factors in non-traditional students' applications, including creativity, written and verbal communication skills, and critical thinking/problem solving ability. Recruiters and hiring managers frequently mention these skills when asked what they look for when hiring new employees, and these also happen to be strengths of many homeschoolers whose uncommon learning experiences have given them the opportunity to develop these skills. Looking for evidence of these traits during the admissions process can help ensure that students who are admitted have the skills necessary to be successful during their four years on campus and highly employable upon graduation.

Educating Others Who Read Homeschoolers' Files

If you have been working full-time in admissions for a while, you may feel that you already have a solid understanding of homeschooling and an effective process for reviewing the applications you receive from homeschoolers. This may not hold true for others new to admissions or only involved part-time, like readers, faculty, and alumni interviewers. Consider including information about homeschooling and the current research on homeschooled students during training sessions, conversations, and other communications or, better yet, provide them with a copy of this book.

Post-Admissions

Reviewing the Process

If you are considering making any changes to your admissions process for homeschoolers, or just want to better understand the experience from their perspective, follow up with some of these students once they arrive on campus. Even a brief, informal conversation may result in some interesting insights about why they applied, what may have been difficult for them, how your process and requirements compare with other schools they applied to, and why they decided to enroll in your school. You may uncover some simple adjustments you could incorporate to reach more homeschoolers and make the process even smoother for your team and the next round of applicants.

Measuring the Results

Admissions is a fast-paced world, full of timelines and deadlines, pressures and commitments, so adding anything new to your already-full list of responsibilities probably is not high on your priority list. However, investing even a small amount of time in tracking how well homeschooled students do, both academically and socially, as they pursue their degree at your school may provide some valuable input into your assessment process. Which students are the most academically successful? Which have taken on leadership roles? What types of job offers do they receive when they graduate? Developing an idea of the key factors that lead to success at your school may help make your recruiting and assessment process even more efficient and effective.

Conclusion

As we have seen, families who homeschool their children do so for a variety of reasons, but they share one thing: they place a high value on education. As such, they are not willing to settle for educational environments and methods that do not sufficiently meet their needs; they are willing to question the status quo and think about new possibilities; and they are personally invested in, and feel accountable for, the results of their educational choices. Unsurprisingly, approximately three-quarters of home educated students between the ages of eighteen and twenty-four continue their education beyond K-12 and pursue college-level coursework.

While a high percentage of homeschoolers have successfully navigated the college admissions process, and have continued to do very well throughout their college careers, many still face unnecessarily difficult and frustrating admissions processes. As a result, many say that they are more likely to look for "homeschool-friendly" colleges where they feel their educational backgrounds will be understood and appreciated, and where accommodating admissions policies, including clear criteria and flexible procedures, allow them to demonstrate what they have accomplished and how they can contribute. Those in higher education who have worked closely with homeschoolers, whether they

> One of the things we've seen from all our data crunching is that GPAs [grade point averages] are worthless as a criteria for hiring, and test scores are worthless . . . Google famously used to ask everyone for a transcript and GPAs and test scores, but we don't anymore, unless you're just a few years out of school. We found that they don't predict anything.
>
> ~Laszlo Bock, Senior VP of People Operations, Google

are admissions counselors, admissions officers, alumni interviewers, or faculty, report that these self-directed, creative, and resourceful students have a lot to offer any community, and are worth recruiting and admitting.

For most homeschoolers, college is just one step on the path to their longer-term goals, not simply the next step after high school. Their personalized education has allowed them to discover their unique strengths and interests, and has also supported them in developing a love of learning that persists into adulthood. Thus, in a quickly moving world which increasingly requires us to become lifelong learners who can keep our knowledge and skills current, homeschoolers are uniquely equipped not only to succeed, but also to lead.

Appendix A

Select Responses to the 2015 National Survey "From Home Education to Higher Education"

The following are selected questions and responses from a national online survey of over 150 homeschooling families representing every region of the United States.

How important are the following college admissions issues to you?

	Highly Important	Average Importance	Least Important
Understanding the application process (e.g., steps, key dates)	67%	30%	3%
Understanding the documentation required (e.g., document types and formats)	90%	6%	3%
Understanding test requirements	87%	10%	3%
Understanding how to apply for scholarships	83%	13%	3%

Other (from comments section)

- Understanding the homeschool portfolio

- College admission for children under the typical high school age
- Application differences for homeschool versus non-homeschooled students
- How tests are changing due to Common Core and how that affects those not using CC curriculum. Is there a specific test homeschoolers should or should not take?
- Special needs accommodations

What would make the college application process easier for homeschooled students?

	Responses
A checklist for the application process	73%
A sample homeschool transcript	77%
A dedicated liaison or counselor	57%
Admissions workshops for homeschoolers	60%
A dedicated page on the college website for homeschoolers	80%

Other (from comments section):

- Clear expectations of what to include in the transcript and course descriptions
- Specify how to complete the Common App. For example, do they want a guidance counselor evaluation done by the parent? Course descriptions? Homeschool philosophy?
- Make clearer exactly what standards should be met and have a counselor or admissions officer to guide and work with homeschooled applicants
- An admission information package for homeschool parents, listing acceptable transcripts and college entry tests
- Opportunities to provide portfolios or essays or other proof of learning and achievements
- Openness to a wide variety of transcript formats
- Clarity about transfer credits and the like; e.g., will taking classes at community college place students out of entrance/freshman financial aid and experience?

- The ability to talk to someone in person: Standardized forms often simply do not work as a summary of a homeschooler's academic achievements.

If there were one thing you would like admissions officers to know about homeschooled students, what would it be?

- Homeschooled students are self-motivated, curious, and have great social skills. They are involved in academic classes, clubs, sports, and the arts. They leave the house frequently!

- Instead of viewing homeschoolers as possibly sheltered, insular, and lacking socialization, please consider that they are actually better socialized and more mature [than traditional school students].

- Homeschoolers are engaged and inquisitive students. They are a diverse group whose unique experience would make a significant contribution to the campus population and to campus life. Many of them have grown up with the opportunity to interact with community members that students in schools do not usually have the time or chance to cross paths with, through jobs, volunteer work, and civic engagement.

- I would like them to be more open-minded and not so judgmental of homeschooled students. I have found they hear "homeschooled" and automatically assume my kids are awkward and uninformed and not ready for the real world.

- The commonality is that we have all made education a significant focus in our families.

- I've never met a homeschooled child who wasn't above grade level compared to public school peers and who wasn't very mature. Homeschooled children are able to spend more time on academics and, with the benefit of one-on-one instruction, learn to be more independent and confident.

- Just because their schooling isn't traditional brick-and-mortar doesn't mean they aren't smart/educated, and they shouldn't be made to jump through extra hoops.

- Homeschooled children are socially active people who take part in many group activities. They are often taught one-on-one and therefore have a strong understanding of what they learn. They are every bit as prepared for college as any child who attended a brick-and-mortar school.

- I think it is important to understand that homeschooling is not the "easy way." This tends to be a big misconception of a lot of people, not just colleges/universities. It is about individualizing the learning to the student rather than the student to the curriculum.

- I would like them to know that homeschoolers' experience and college readiness can vary greatly. If they encounter a homeschooled student who is poorly prepared, I would like them to keep an open mind and realize there are others who are fully or more prepared than average.

- The fact that our high school transcripts may differ in the types of courses does not indicate our students are not "college ready." If anything, it means they've already had a chance to explore different subjects, and may be more aware of what they want to study.

If you could ask an admissions officer any question, what would it be?

- What do you see in homeschool students that you value?

- How do you decide if you will admit a homeschool child? Are there certain things you are looking for that make the decision an easy yes or no?

- What advantages do you think homeschoolers have in the admission process? What disadvantages?

- How do you feel about homeschooling personally?

- What are the most important things for homeschoolers to put together? Are there types of exams and classes that are preferable (e.g., AP versus CLEP versus SAT Subject Tests)?

- How can my child best demonstrate that s/he is a top-notch applicant?

- Is there someone on staff who will advocate for admission for my homeschool student, someone with experience with homeschoolers who can translate our experience into "educationese"?

- How can we best communicate our academic experience, knowledge and life lessons so that you can apply them to your entrance requirements?

Appendix B:

List of Resources for Additional Information

<u>Homeschooling and Alternative Education Websites</u>

Alternative Education Resource Association (AERO)

A hub of communications and support for educational alternatives around the world.

www.educationrevolution.org

Alternatives to School

Discover more about home-based, self-directed learning, community resource centers, and democratic schools.

www.alternativestoschool.com

GHF: Gifted Homeschoolers Forum

A forum that supports, educates, and advocates for gifted and twice-exceptional children, their families, and the professionals who serve them in the United States and around the world.

www.giftedhomeschoolers.org

Home School Legal Defense Association (HSLDA)

A nonprofit advocacy organization established to defend and advance the constitutional right of parents to direct the education of their children and to protect family freedoms.

www.hslda.org

Homeschool Central

The place to find all of the homeschool resources you need including curriculum choices, support groups, and how to homeschool.

www.homeschoolcentral.com

Homeschool.com

Homeschooling curriculum and homeschool resources for beginning or advanced homeschoolers.

www.homeschool.com

Homeschooling Today

A magazine is dedicated to the encouragement of families and parents who are educating at home.

www.homeschoolingtoday.com

Institute for Democratic Education in America (IDEA)

IDEA is a national effort to connect education with and through our nation's democratic values.

www.democraticeducation.org

National Alliance of Secular Homeschoolers (NASH)

An organization created to advance the recognition of secular education in the homeschooling community and to support academically secular homeschoolers.

nationalallianceofsecularhomeschoolers.wordpress.com

National Home Education Research Institute

NHERI conducts and collects research about homeschooling (home-based education, home schooling), and publishes the research journal called the *Home School Researcher*.

www.nheri.org

Secular Eclectic Academic (SEA) Homeschoolers

A friendly place for secular homeschoolers where they can chat, ask questions, and find other like-minded homeschoolers.

www.seahomeschoolers.com

Secular Homeschool

An online destination for secular, eclectic, non-religious, inclusive, free-thinking homeschoolers.

www.secularhomeschool.com

Teach Your Own (the author's site)

Provides ideas, tools, research, and resources to parents and families with the goal of helping all children develop to their full intellectual, emotional, social, and creative potential.

www.teachyourown.org

The Uncommon Applicant

A community of experienced college counselors and advisors ready to assist non-traditional students with all aspects of the college admissions process. Check out their list of "homeschool-friendly" colleges at www.uncommonapplicant.com/resources/.

www.uncommonapplicant.com

<u>Homeschooling Conferences</u>

A2Z Homeschooling

http://a2zhomeschooling.com/events/

Great Homeschool Conventions

www.greathomeschoolconventions.com

Home Education Resources and Information

www.herijax.com

Homeschool Association of California

www.hscconference.com

North East Homeschool Convention

www.northeasthomeschoolconvention.com

Northeast Unschooling Conference

www.northeastunschoolingconference.com

Pacific Northwest Homeschool College Fair

www.homeschoolcollegefair.com

Southeast Homeschool Expo

www.southeasthomeschoolexpo.com

The Homeschool Mom

www.thehomeschoolmom.com/local-support/homeschool-conventions-conferences-and-events/

The Texas Home School Coalition

www.thsc.org

<u>Books</u>

Dumbing Us Down, John Taylor Gatto (New Society Publishers: 2005)

Forging Paths: Beyond Traditional Schooling, Wes Beach (GHF Press: 2012)

Guerrilla Learning, Grace Llewellyn (John Wiley & Sons, Inc.: 2001

Homeschooled Teens, Sue Patterson (2nd Tier Publishing: 2015)

Making the Choice: When Typical School Doesn't Fit Your Atypical Child, Corin Goodwin and Mika Gustavson (GHF Press: 2011)

Punished by Rewards, Alfie Kohn (Houghton Mifflin Harcourt Publishing Company: 1993)

Self-Directed Learning: Documentation and Life Stories, Wes Beach (GHF Press: 2015)

Teach Your Own, John Holt and Pat Farenga (Da Capo Press, Perseus Books Group: 2003)

Wounded by School, Kirsten Olson (Teachers College Press: 2009)

Videos/Documentaries

Class Dismissed Movie

www.youtube.com/user/ClassDismissedMovie

Do Schools Kill Creativity? (TED Talk)

www.youtube.com/watch?v=iG9CE55wbtY

Hackschooling Makes Me Happy (TED Talk)

www.youtube.com/watch?v=h11u3vtcpaY

Self-Directed Learning Fundamentals

www.youtube.com/watch?v=YoE480mzrk0

Sudbury Valley School—Focus and Intensity

www.youtube.com/user/SudburyValley

Endnotes

Introduction

1. Jeremy Redford, Danielle Battle, and Stacey Bielick, "Homeschooling in the United States: 2012," Institute of Education Sciences: National Center for Education Statistics, US Department of Education (April 2017). Accessed January 8, 2016. https://nces.ed.gov/pubs2016/2016096rev.pdf.

2. Redford, Battle, and Bielick, "Homeschooling in the United States: 2012."

3. Brian D. Ray, "Academic Achievement and Demographic Traits of Homeschool Students: A Nationwide Study," *Academic Leadership Live: The Online Journal*, vol. 8, no. 1 (Winter 2010). Accessed January 22, 2016. http://www.nheri.org/AcademicAchievementAndDemographicTraitsOfHomeschoolStudentsRay2010.pdf.

4. Brian D. Ray, PhD, "2.04 Homeschool Students in the United States in 2010," *National Home Education Research Institute* (January 3, 2011). Accessed January 22, 2016. https://www.nheri.org/HomeschoolPopulationReport2010.pdf.

5. Peter Gray, "A Survey of Grown Unschoolers I: Overview of Findings," *Psychology Today*, June 7, 2014. Accessed January 27, 2016. https://www.psychologytoday.com/blog/freedom-learn/201406/survey-grown-unschoolers-i-overview-findings.

Chapter One

1. Ama Mazama and Garvey Lundy, "African American Homeschooling as Racial Protectionism," *Journal of Black Studies*, vol. 43, no. 77 (October 2012): 24.

2. Jessica Huseman, "The Rise of Homeschooling Among Black Families," *The Atlantic* (February 17, 2015). Accessed February 5, 2016. https://www.theatlantic.com/education/archive/2015/02/the-rise-of-homeschooling-among-black-families/385543/.

3. Emma Brown, "Yale Study Suggests Racial Bias Among Preschool Teachers," *The Washington Post* (September 27, 2016). Accessed September 30, 2016. https://www.washingtonpost.com/news/education/wp/2016/09/27/yale-study-suggests-racial-bias-among-preschool-teachers/?utm_term=.05bb2a3f7722.

4. Corin Barsily Goodwin, Martha Shaindlin, Emily Villamar, and Madeline Goodwin, "US Public Education Policy: Missing Voices," *Issue Lab* (May 20, 2017). Accessed May 23, 2017. http://www.issuelab.org/resource/us_public_education_policy_missing_voices.

5. Matthew Lieberman, "Education and the Social Brain," *Trends in Neuroscience and Education*, 1 (2012) 3-9 (July 10, 2012). Accessed March 18, 2016. http://www.scn.ucla.edu/pdf/Lieberman(2012)TINE.pdf.

6. "Gallup Student Poll 2014" *Gallup* (2014). Accessed September 30, 2016. http://www.gallup.com/services/180029/gallup-student-poll-2014-overall-report.aspx.

Chapter Two

1. Peter Gray and Gina Riley, "The Challenges and Benefits of Unschooling, According to 232 Families Who Have Chosen that Route," *Journal of Unschooling and Alternative Learning*, vol. 7, no. 14 (2013): 1.

2. Gray and Riley, "The Challenges and Benefits of Unschooling, According to 232 Families Who Have Chosen that Route," 14.

3. Peter Gray and David Chanoff, "Democratic Schooling: What Happens to Young People Who Have Charge of Their Own Education?," *American Journal of Education* (University of Chicago, February 1986): 182.

Chapter Three

1. Richard Medlin, "Homeschooling and the Question of Socialization Revisited," *Peabody Journal of Education*, vol. 88, no. 3 (2013).

2. Sue Patterson, *Homeschooled Teens: 75 Young People Speak About Their Lives Without School* (Wimberley, TX: 2nd Tier Publishing, 2015): 83.

3. Paul Jones and Gene Gloeckner, "A Study of Admissions Officers' Perceptions of and Attitudes Toward Homeschool Students," *The Journal of College Admission* (Fall 2004): 18.

4.   "America's Changing Religious Landscape," *Pew Research Center: Religion & Public Life* (May 12, 2015). Accessed March 31, 2016. http://www.pewforum.org/2015/05/12/americas-changing-religious-landscape/.

5.   Redford, Battle, and Bielick, "Homeschooling in the United States: 2012."

6.   Laura Vanderkam, "How These Parents Work and Homeschool, Too," *Fast Company* (January 20, 2016). Accessed February 5, 2016. https://www.fastcompany.com/3055528/second-shift/how-these-parents-work-and-homeschool-too.

7.   Brian D. Ray, PhD, "Research Facts on Homeschooling," *National Home Education Research Institute* (March 23, 2016). Accessed April 8, 2016. http://www.nheri.org/research/research-facts-on-homeschooling.html.

8.   Ray, PhD, "Academic Achievement and Demographic Traits of Homeschool Students."

Chapter Four

1.   Jones and Gloeckner, "A Study of Admissions Officers' Perceptions of and Attitudes Toward Homeschool Students": 18.

Chapter Five

1.   David McGrath, "What Changed This Teacher's Mind About Homeschooling," *Chicago Tribune* (February 18, 2016). Accessed March 25, 2016. http://www.chicagotribune.com/news/opinion/commentary/ct-home-school-education-college-dupage-perspec-0219-jm-20160218-story.html.

2.   Michael F. Cogan, "Exploring Academic Outcomes of Homeschooled Students," *Journal of College Admission* (Summer 2010). Accessed January 22, 2016. http://files.eric.ed.gov/fulltext/EJ893891.pdf.

3.   Mary Beth Bolle-Brummond and Roger D. Wessel, "Homeschooled students in college: Background influences, college integration, and environmental pull factors," *Journal of Research in Education*, 22(1) (Spring 2012).

4.   Dawn Meza Soufleris, "From Home to Hall: The Transitional Experiences of Homeschooled Students Entering Residential University Settings" (doctoral dissertation, State University of New York: 2014). Accessed March 24, 2016. http://pqdtopen.proquest.com/doc/1511452650.html?FMT=AI.

5.   Paul May, "Listening to the Freshman Voice: First-Year Self-Efficacy and College Expectations Based on High School Types" (doctoral dissertation, University of

North Texas: 2013). Accessed March 24, 2016. https://digital.library.unt.edu/ark:/67531/metadc271863/m2/1/high_res_d/dissertation.pdf.

6. Gary Mason, "Homeschool Recruiting: Lessons Learned on the Journey," *The Journal of College Admission* (Fall 2004). Accessed April 8, 2016. http://www.ahem.info/Documents/JournalofCollegeAdmissionFall04.pdf.

7. Brian Ray, PhD, "Homeschooling Grows Up," *Home School Legal Defense Association* (2003). Accessed April 8, 2016. https://www.hslda.org/research/ray2003/HomeschoolingGrowsUp.pdf.

8. Peter Gray, "A Survey of Grown Unschoolers II: Going on to College," *Psychology Today* (June 17, 2014). Accessed January 27, 2016. https://www.psychologytoday.com/blog/freedom-learn/201406/survey-grown-unschoolers-ii-going-college.

Chapter Six

1. "Gallup Student Poll 2014."

2. "Basic Eligibility Criteria: Ability-to-benefit Alternatives," *Federal Student Aid: An Office of the US Department of Education*. Accessed September 30, 2016. https://studentaid.ed.gov/sa/eligibility/basic-criteria#ability-to-benefit.

3. HSDLA Legal Staff, "Federal Requirements for Homeschoolers Seeking College Admission and Financial Aid," *HSDLA: Current Issue Analysis* (October 2010). Accessed September 30, 2016. http://www.hslda.org/docs/nche/000000/College_Federal_Aid2010.pdf.

4. HSDLA Legal Staff, "Federal Requirements for Homeschoolers Seeking College Admission and Financial Aid."

Acknowledgments

This book would not be nearly what it is without the personal stories shared by Korie and Max, Karin and Jack, Wendy, and Mickelle. I am so grateful to each of you for taking the time to share your families' very personal stories with me, and am inspired by the strength and bravery you and your families have shown through times of uncertainty and struggle. Likewise, I am incredibly grateful to Nicole Jobson for sharing both her personal and professional experiences in guiding homeschoolers through the college admissions process, and for helping me clarify my understanding and explanation of some of the details of federal homeschooling regulations.

Additionally, I owe an enormous amount of thanks to the admissions officers who took the time to participate in our national survey and respond to my email requests and questions. I am most especially grateful to those who allowed me to interview them, sharing valuable insights, ideas, and recommendations. I hope this book proves to be a valuable resource to each of you.

To the broader homeschooling community, I thank you for your continued feedback and encouragement as I peppered you with questions and requests for input throughout this project. I hope I have represented our community well, and that the results of this effort help make the path to higher education and beyond a little smoother for all our kids.

Finally, and perhaps most of all, I am grateful to the staff and volunteers at GHF: Gifted Homeschoolers Forum and GHF Press, specifically Corin Barsily Goodwin and Sarah J. Wilson, for providing me with the opportunity and support to write and share this book—a years-long personal goal.

About the Author

Lori Dunlap worked for nearly twenty years in the corporate world, first as a management consultant to Fortune 500 companies, and then at a large research university as a career development program director and adjunct faculty member. In 2010 she decided to make a radical life change and left her job to begin homeschooling her two sons. In addition, she has been researching and writing about education and parenting issues, and working with homeschooling families as an education and career advisor. You can connect with and find out more about her current projects at:

Website: www.teachyourown.org
Facebook: @TeachYourOwn
Twitter: @NWDunlap

Made in the USA
Middletown, DE
17 November 2018